Set up a Therapy Business:

A step-by-step guide

by Gill Warren

Set up a Therapy Business: A step-by-step guide
by Gill Warren

First Edition 2010

Copyright © Ethical Business Publishing 2010

First published in the United Kingdom in 2010 by
Ethical Business Publishing
40 Backwell Hill Road, Backwell, Bristol BS48 3PL
www.setupatherapybusiness.com

Some names used in the examples of this book have been changed to protect the identity of those individuals.

ISBN 978-0-9566282-0-6

A CIP catalogue record for this book is available from the British Library.

Book production by The Choir Press: www.thechoirpress.co.uk
Cover design and book layout by G&T Design: www.g-and-t.com

Contents

Module 1: It's All About You
Are you ready to set up in business? 7

Exercise 1 | Exercise 2A: a questionnaire | Exercise 2B: How will you know you are successful as
a therapist in business? | Strengths & Weaknesses | Your Action Plan to Overcome Weaknesses |
The Nine Main Reasons that Business Fail | Business Failures: Therapists | The Eight Reasons Given
by Therapists Why they are Not in Business Three Years after Qualification | Business Successes:
Therapists | The Ten Reasons Given by Successful Therapists Why They Are Successful | Summary

Module 2: Is There Anyone Out There?
Market research 17

Which niche to choose? | Who Pays the Piper? | Market research: what is there already? | Step-by-
Step Guide to Market Research | Step 1: who else is out there? | Step 2: compare and contrast |
Step 3: gather your information while you may! | Step 4: into the lion's den... | Step 5: assess your
competitors' strengths and weaknesses | Step 6: work out your Unique Selling Proposition (USP)
| An example—my USP | An example of how your USP may look | Market research – what is the
demand? | Desk research | Useful Internet sites | Field research | Tips for Compiling Questionnaires
| Interviewing experts | Ten Tips for a Questionnaire | An example questionnaire | Analysing the
results | Summary

Module 3: What Shape Should you Take?
Legal form 37

The features of a Sole Trader: advantages, disadvantages | The features of a General Partnership:
advantages, disadvantages | The features of a Limited Liability Partnership | The features of a
Limited Company: advantages, disadvantages | The usual form for therapists | Ten Steps to Set Up
as a Sole Trader | More resources | Summary

Module 9: Please Sir, can I have some more?

Finance

Short-term Finance | Overdrafts | Long-term Finance | Family or Friends loan (or Self Financed) | Bank Loan | Grants | Advantages and Disadvantages of Different Finance | Loans from friends or family | Bank Loans | Bank Overdrafts | Lease/HP | Other Finance Forms | Current Position for Obtaining Finance | Taking a Business Plan to Finance Providers | What are the Investors or Bank looking for? | Ongoing monitoring by the banks | Summary

Module 10: Become a Client Magnet

Marketing

What is Marketing? | How do you do Effective Marketing? | Test All Your Marketing | What are the best sort of testimonials? | Tips for testing and measuring promotional costs | Six tips to increase the effectiveness of advertising in print | Relationship Marketing | Alternative ("Guerrilla") Marketing | Testimonials | Maximise Different Income Streams | Links to Other Websites | Focus on Customers' Problems with a Multi-Discipline Approach | Sell Other Services or Products to Your Existing Clients | Some "Dos And Don'ts" of Selling | How to convert an enquiry by telephone or face-to-face | Marketing Strategy | Exercise 1—Client Analysis | Exercise 2—Self Analysis | How Do You Attract Clients? | Bonus Extra Tips To Help Increase Your Sales And Obtain More Customers | Summary

Module 11: Communication

Website and internet marketing

Website Communication | Opportunities for affiliation | Write blogs, articles and books to sell or give away | Choose your domain name carefully | Use keywords in the website pages | Search engine optimisation | Other tactics | Summary

Module 12: Keeping Score

Record-keeping and accounts

Why Do You Need To Keep Records? | Basic Records You Must Keep | Companies | Money coming in | Money going out | General Tips on Bookkeeping | Petty Cash | Monthly accounts | Bank Reconciliation | Filing | Preparing Accounts | Employees | Wages Records | VAT | Summary

Module 13: Pay Your Dues

Introduction to Income Tax for the self-employed

Registering for Tax and National Insurance | National Insurance | Tax Calculations | Examples of allowable and non-allowable expenditure | Summary

Preface

Margaret Gray

This book is essential if you are considering embarking on a fulfilling career as a therapist, or if you are already a practicing therapist and wish to ensure that you are working optimally for your personal fulfilment and best income. In ensuring that your practice stays healthy and continues to blossom and expand you will minimise the avoidable risk of burnout due to overworking and low earnings.

As therapists we are all aware that in this time of unprecedented change and evolution on our planet, an increasing number of people are coming to our practice, seeking support, guidance, information and healing. In challenging the concept of a nine-to-five job with a secure pension, the current economic changes have also enabled more people to seek a vocation versus a job. Hence, for many, the dream of becoming a self-employed therapist has finally become a real possibility.

However, for those of us who train or re-train as therapists, without a business background, the greatest challenge is often in applying our desire to heal and work with people to the practicalities of running an effective business and earning a good living. I remember being so excited at doing what I felt most passionate about when I first set up my astrology practice, that I was reluctant to charge for my services. I also had no idea how to market and advertise my skills, what to do re my taxes and never even considered doing a business plan or researching who my clients might be! In fact coming from a statutory Social Work background I struggled with even feeling that I deserved to earn a good income doing what I most enjoyed doing, forgetting that if my bills did not get paid, I would have to go back to a job I no longer found fulfilling!

My work life changed radically when I met and set up a holistic therapy business in 2000 with the author of this wonderful guide, Gill Warren. I immediately trusted Gill's extensive business background as well as her practical and compassionate approach to running a business and over the four years of co-owning and running the school, Gill patiently took me through all the steps in her guide. As we applied each of them, the business grew from a neglected small school of holistic therapies, to a thriving business with an excellent reputation all over the UK and beyond. Applying what I learnt through Gill's mentoring in our joint business, to my own Astrology and healing practice enabled me to base myself in my dream home in Hawaii, working internationally as a Psychological Astrologer, Vocational coach and Master Reiki practitioner and teacher. Hence, I can truly say, hand on heart, that each and every one of the principles in this guide works.

From my own experience and the feedback from students in the four years I co-owned the holistic therapy school with Gill I cannot recommend Gill's work highly enough as it is based on knowledge, experience, authenticity and integrity. Since selling the school Gill has continued to teach and expand the material in this guide for over 9 years to therapists from a variety of backgrounds both in the form of workshops and coaching sessions. I truly envisage that this book will become a core textbook on all therapy courses. I also highly recommend coaching sessions with Gill if you are considering setting up a therapy practice or if you would like to ensure that your current practice is working at its optimum.

Margaret Gray
www.astrologypsychological.com

Disclaimer

This publication is defined to provide accurate and authoritative information in relation to the subject matter. The views expressed in this book are those of the author, but they are general views only, and readers are urged to consult a qualified specialist for individual advice in particular situations. The author and publisher accept no responsibility for any consequences, arising directly or indirectly, from advice given herein.

This book is not intended as a substitute for financial or legal advice. It is sold on the understanding that the publisher and author are not engaged in rendering legal, accounting or other professional services. All the legal and financial information presented in this book relates to English jurisdiction and was correct at the time of going to press (in 2010). Where possible, website addresses have been given so that you can check the latest information.

Most of the modules apply whichever jurisdiction you are in; however, for detailed legal and financial advice in your country you will need to contact the appropriate authorities in your country for pertinent legal and financial advice.

Introduction:

What's it all about?

Welcome to this step-by-step guide to setting up a therapy business. I really hope that you will find this very useful as it is stuffed with lots of templates and practical advice.

There are some really good resources out there that tell you what to do to set up a business (and I will share some of the links and resources with you), but very few that show you how to do it. There are even fewer that are relevant to therapy businesses and I will certainly share those I have found to be useful.

There is also a growing collection of "how to" videos which you can watch on YouTube/Viddler as a video course. For this you look over my shoulder as I show you how to do various things such as preparing a cash flow forecast or registering online as self-employed. Eventually I will put these together into a DVD that you can access from home if you don't have a computer. For more information, check out my websites, www.setupatherapybusiness.com and www.growyourtherapybusiness.com

If there are particular aspects of setting up a business you would like me to cover, please email me at gefwarren@gmail.com and I will do what I can to cover it by way of blog or video as appropriate.

Is it relevant to your therapy?

Therapies can be said to fall into three basic categories:

"Biomechanical" type therapies such as osteopathy, physiotherapy, Alexander Technique. These therapies are often regulated by law and therapists can be employed by the National Health Service in the UK, although most are self-employed.

"Talking" therapies such as the various forms of psychotherapy, psychodynamic therapy, Jungian analysis, Neuro Linguistic Programming (NLP), counselling, hypnosis and life coaching. The UK Government is seeking to regulate the psychotherapy profession in particular by making Cognitive Behavioural Therapy the "standard" and the one available through the NHS. Most therapists in this category are self-employed (even if they are under the NHS).

"Energy" therapies, that covers a range from acupuncture and reiki, through to various forms of massage, reflexology and shamanism. Most therapists under this category are self-employed.

This book is set to cover the three basic sorts of category and when you are going through you can think how you will adapt it for your therapy. If you need more specific advice on how an area relates to your particular therapy please email me on gefwarren@gmail.com and I will attempt to cover it in a video or article as appropriate.

So who am I, and why should you listen to me?

My name is Gill Warren; I am a business coach and chartered accountant and have co-owned and run my own successful businesses (including a therapy business).

I have also taught business to therapists for the last nine years, as well as being the grateful recipient of many therapies for most of my adult life, so I have a lot of experience in the area.

In order to bring you the widest range of experiences to learn from, I have also badgered various friends and colleagues for their experiences and all of this is put together so you can benefit from it.

What are the Steps for Setting up a Business?

Well, if you have already qualified in your chosen therapy, the steps you need to go through in order to set up a business are as follows:

Step 1: It's All About You

Are you ready to go into business? This will need some self-analysis to find out your strengths and weaknesses and how you are going to overcome those weaknesses. This is also the ideal time to find out if you are "cut out" to be a business person. This will be covered in **Module 1**.

Step 2: Is There Anyone Out There?

You may be the most brilliant therapist ever but is there anyone out there who wants your services and are they prepared to buy? There is only one way to find out and that is to carry out market research. This will be covered in **Module 2**.

Step 3: What Shape Should you Take?

Before you start you will need to think about which legal form you take to trade through and what business name you will adopt. This is covered in **Module 3**.

Step 4: Licence to Heal

Before you set up you need to consider what licences you need and the insurances. All a little tedious but very necessary. **Module 4** covers regulations and insurances and health and safety requirements.

Step 5: You Need a Cunning Little Plan

Every business owner should write a business plan to work out whether you have a feasible business and if you are applying for funding your business investors or banks will expect to see a plan and for you to deliver the results as forecast. We cover the contents of a business plan in **Module 5**.

Step 6: Location, Location, Location

Are you going to work from home, or a clinic, or are you going to be mobile? Or maybe a mixture of them? How do you choose where you need to be? We look at the various pros and cons of the various choices in **Module 6**.

Step 7: Money, Money, Money

How are you going to set your fees? Are you going to position yourself at the top end of the market or are you going to offer a range of fees depending on your clients' circumstances. In **Module 7** I show you a formula for working out a minimum fee per session.

Step 8: Long Live the King

"Cash is King" – it is the lifeblood of a business and without it you will go out of business very quickly. So you need to know how to forecast it and control it to give yourself a successful business. In **Module 8** we look at a simple cash flow forecast, and how you can manage the cash in your business.

Step 9: "Please Sir, Can I Have Some More?"

Having completed your cash flow forecast you may find that you need some more funds... where do you go to get it and how much will it cost you? In **Module 9** we look at where you can go to obtain finance for your business and some tips for what banks and investors are looking for when you present your case.

Step 10: Become a Client Magnet

How do you market your business to get people beating a path to your door? Perhaps the trickiest part of any business but it's all about long term relationships not a quick win. **Module 10** is all about how to attract all those wonderful clients who will just love to come to use your services.

Step 11: Communication

Do you need a website? Yes, yes, yes. The internet offers a real potential for therapists and very few have successfully exploited it fully. In **Module 11** I show you how you can set up and some tactics for extra income streams.

Step 12: Keeping Score

Okay, you may say you hate numbers, but in **Module 12** I show you how you can easily keep simple accounts that will be acceptable for managing the business and keeping the taxman happy (always a good idea!)

Step 13: Pay your Dues

In **Module 13**, I show you how you can register for taxes, what sort of expenses are allowable against your tax bill, and where you can get the latest information.

Step 14: Ready for Takeoff

Like an airline pilot before take off you need to go through various checklists and in **Module 14** I walk you through those checklists to make sure you have considered various areas before hurtling down the runway.

Well, I hope you have checked the emergency exits and you are sitting comfortably with your safety belt on, ready to head off to your destination. Enjoy the ride!

Module 1: It's All About You
Are You Ready to Set up in Business?

Not everyone has the aptitude or attitude to set up in business on their own. Inexperience does not need to be a barrier, and reading books and doing courses like this help to give you some of the knowledge and skills to set up and run a successful business.

So, you've finished your therapy training course. Now what? It is probably worth spending a little time having an honest and objective look at your skills and knowledge as of today to see what you need to look at and either buy in, train for or perhaps go into partnership with someone with a complementary skill set.

Exercise 1

Think about the person that you consider being a very successful business person. If it helps, think of a particular person who you believe is successful in business, for example Richard Branson.

Now, think about the qualities that you consider are necessary to be a successful therapist. Again, if it helps, think of a particular person that you believe is a successful therapist.

Did you find similar qualities between the two people?

For a successful businessperson, you would expect these qualities to include:

1. independent, including being able to tolerate working on your own, with no certainty or set routines
2. self-motivated, with an aim to achieve and maintain high standards
3. finance-orientated, being aware of your income and costs, including your personal time
4. a risk taker and opportunistic, seeing opportunities for additional income streams (for example perhaps selling products to your clients)
5. organised
6. self-confident
7. proactive
8. committed, dedicated and willing to make some personal sacrifices
9. being good at setting goals, and managing to goals
10. resilient: you will do whatever it takes to achieve what you have set out to do
11. indefatigable: working long hours, sometimes writing up books/ dealing with paperwork and phone calls late in the evening on a regular basis?

For a successful therapist the qualities that you expect are being:

1. caring
2. professional
3. organised
4. proactive
5. self-confident
6. have strong ethics and integrity
7. passionate about what you do

There are of course many other qualities that one would expect from a businessperson and a therapist. Some of the qualities are shared and others seem to contradict each other: for example being finance orientated and caring. The key is to get a balance between the two. In order to be a successful therapist in business, you need to be both caring and concerned about the "bottom line", which is jargon for profit, being the excess of income over costs.

Exercise 2

It is important to work out why you're going into business and what you want from business. Answer these questions as honestly and objectively as possible. Sometimes it is useful to get a close friend or family member to complete it about you too.

Part A: a questionnaire

Do you intend to make as much money as possible?   *Yes/no*

Are you prepared to work long hours?   *Yes/no*

Are you prepared to forgo or cut down on holiday?   *Yes/no*

Are you prepared to work most evenings and at weekends?   *Yes/no*

Can you cope with stress and uncertainty?   *Yes/no*

Do you have the support of your family?   *Yes/no*

Are you prepared to work on your own?   *Yes/no*

Do you enjoy being responsible for what you achieve?   *Yes/no*

Do you enjoy independence?   *Yes/no*

Are you prepared to take risks?   *Yes/no*

Do you persist even though things are tough?   *Yes/no*

Do you recognize when you need help?   *Yes/no*

*Can you distinguish between items that are important
and those that are urgent?*   *Yes/no*

To be successful in business you need to have a majority of "yes" answers to the above questionnaire.

If in your answers you are not prepared to be flexible, work hard, with unsociable hours, are not prepared to work on your own or cannot cope with stress and uncertainty perhaps now is the time to reconsider whether you really do want to set up in business.

Part B: How will you know you are successful as a therapist in business?

Will it be a number of successful outcomes for clients?

Will it be earning a certain amount per year?

Will it be to achieve a certain number of clients in the year?

How many clients do you want by the end of year one?

How much money do you want to make by the end of year one after all costs including taxes?

How will you know when your clients have a successful outcome?

The more details you have and set out your criteria for success, the easier it will be to measure against that criteria and will be very helpful in completing your business plan in a later module.

A number of therapists consider themselves to be successful by working on their therapy one or two days a week and earning enough to cover holiday money, giving them the flexibility to spend more time with their family. Others are working full time and supporting themselves completely and are equally successful.

Exercise 3

Strengths

List down your personal strengths and knowledge. This can cover both professional and other traits that will be useful in business.

Weaknesses

List down your personal weaknesses and areas of gaps in your knowledge. This can also cover both professional and other traits that will be useful in business.

Your Action Plan to Overcome Weaknesses

What actions can you take to overcome each of the weaknesses noted above?

Why do Businesses Fail?

The UK government produces statistics that show that after three years, forty per cent of businesses fail. Having mentoring and training (such as through a business coaching programme) increases your chance of success: research shows there is a twenty per cent improvement of chances in business if training and advice is taken at the onset, measured after three years.

The Nine Main Reasons that Business Fail

The Small Business Administration in the USA state that the key factors for small businesses failing are as follows:

1. **Over-expansion.** Businesses grow too quickly or take on more fixed costs than they can cover by their turnover (sales).
2. **Poor capital structure.** Businesses take on too much debt and cannot meet the interest and capital repayments.
3. **Overspending.** Businesses do not control their costs or look for the cheapest deals. It is very easy at the outset to underestimate the various costs involved. Research into costs, seeking advice from advisors or mentors, and preparing and managing to a very detailed business plan help to mitigate this problem.
4. **Lack of the reserve funding.** Businesses do not have sufficient funds in reserve to cope with the volatility of increased costs such as energy bills, or delays in receiving cash from customers.
5. **Poor location.** You need to consider accessibility to your market and your competition. It is too easy to be tempted by cheap rent in a poor location, but if your target market is for the more affluent, they are unlikely to make the journey to a poor location.

6. **Ineffective marketing and self-promotion.** There is no point in being the best therapist in the world if nobody knows of your existence.
7. **Underestimating the competition.** It will take time to build your reputation and just because a competitor has a very good business in a certain location, it does not mean you will be able to replicate the same business success.
8. **Poor customer service.** In order to get repeat business you need to have good customer service and build a good reputation.
9. **Poor internal controls.** A number of businesses do not prepare an adequate business plan and manage their business to that business plan; in particular businesses need to be able to control their cash flow.

How to improve in these areas will be covered in later modules of the workbook and in the video series.

Business Failures: Therapists

In research that I have done of therapists three years after their training, more than half had either not set up a business in the first place or had stopped trading. The sample was quite small, less than 100 people, so it cannot be extrapolated to the general population, but their reasons are interesting.

The Eight Reasons Given by Therapists Why they are Not in Business Three Years after Qualification

The reasons given as to why they had not continued or started trading are set out below:

1. Personal Development. They did the course for their own personal development, rather than to set up in business.
2. Skills in other jobs. They intended to use the skills that they picked up in their existing jobs (for example as nurses) rather than going into business.

3. Lack of support. They did not get the support they needed from their family or partner, particularly working in the evenings and at weekends, or giving up a regular second income.
4. Poor market research. They did not do sufficient market research in the first place to find out who their competitors were and the demand for their services.
5. Poor marketing. They did insufficient marketing or self-promotion in the first place to build up a potential client base.
6. Needing additional skills. In order to retain clients they needed to build up additional skills and offer other therapies. For various reasons they did not want to or could not afford to take up further training.
7. Poor cash control. They underestimated the costs of running the business and overestimated the number of clients they could achieve. My experience is that in the first year income is half that predicted and costs twice the amount predicted.
8. Commitment. They had to give up too much: their socialising time, their job perks/pension or sick and holiday pay benefits.

Well I hope this hasn't put you off too much! If you are prepared to do the flip side of all the above, it gives you an idea of how to avoid failure:
1. Treat it as a business,
2. Obtain support from your family,
3. Do market research,
4. Spend sufficient time on marketing (initially maybe as much as eighty per cent)
5. Find out what other services your customers want and see what you can do to secure those services (either through training yourself or bringing in different therapists)
6. Be ruthless with your cost management, especially initially. Ask yourself for every pound that you spend, "Do I really need to spend this?"

Business Successes: Therapists

I also asked those therapists who considered themselves to be successful what they thought contributed to that success.

The Ten Reasons Given by Successful Therapists Why They Are Successful

For those therapists who were successful (by their criteria of success) the reasons given are as below:

1. Good marketing. Spending sustained time and effort (possibly about a day a week) to market and promote themselves.
2. Reputation. Building up a reputation by always delivering or over delivering on the service provided.
3. Selling more products or services to current clients. Providing additional services or products, for example sales of aromatherapy oils and lotions.
4. Becoming an expert. Building up their reputation by becoming "an expert" by writing articles or books, teaching and running courses, giving talks, or sitting on the local or national therapy councils.
5. Having additional income streams Looking to build different income streams, or working part-time whilst they built up a client base.
6. Flexibility of location or time. Being flexible, for example having a clinic in different places on different days of the week, or being available at the time best suited to their target market.
7. Getting cross referrals. Starting off half or one day a week in a clinic that already has a good reputation, offering a therapy not already covered in that clinic, thereby getting cross referrals.
8. Managing costs. Being realistic about the income that could be generated and keeping costs as low as possible while maintaining standards and the right image.
9. Cooperation. Working with other therapists in partnership offering a wider range of therapies.
10. Mentoring. Being mentored.

For more information on different coaching programmes, or if you would like individual business coaching, look at my website, http://www.setupatherapybusiness.com or email me: gefwarren@gmail.com

Summary

In this module you should have taken an honest and objective look at your skills and preferences. Not everyone is cut out to cope with the risks and uncertainties of being in business. There's no loss of face to make a decision at this time, that this is not the right path for you, and could save you considerable energy, time and money later.

However, lacking some of the skills that are necessary need not be a deterrent. For example if you hate numbers you can hire a bookkeeper to keep your books for you, although of course it means that you will need to earn more to cover the costs of employing a bookkeeper. Having an objective view of your weaknesses, gives you the opportunity to either build up the necessary skills or attain them from other professionals.

If you enjoy having control over your life, like meeting new people, having a sense of independence and don't mind working hard, then self-employment as a therapist can be an ideal solution for you. Assuming that is you, let's proceed with how to set up in business as a therapist...

Further general resources I recommend you look at:

Business Link: Starting Up <http://www.businesslink.gov.uk/bdotg/action/layer?r.l1=1073858805&r.l3=1075215800&topicId=1073858805&r.lc=en&r.t=RESOURCES&r.i=1075216019&r.l2=1073859137&r.s=m>

The Law Society: Lawyers for your business <http://www.lawsociety.org.uk/choosingandusing/helpyourbusiness/foryourbusiness.law>

Alliance and Leicester Bizguides <https://www.alliance-leicestercommercialbank.co.uk/bizguides/full/index.asp>

Module 2: Is There Anyone Out There?
Market research

Okay, so you've decided to set up in business: now what? If it's going to be more than a hobby you need to find out whether there is actually a market for your services or products. Who will buy, why will they buy from you and how much will they buy? How do you go about doing market research?

Customers buy a product or service because it either solves a problem for them or give them opportunities that they aspire to.

So for example, if you are a chiropractor or osteopath, it is very clear what the need of the customer is—they have a bad back or they are in pain.

For the psychotherapist or counsellor usually people want to work through emotional issues or current trauma.

For the body therapies such as aromatherapy, reflexology, acupuncture and Indian head massage, there may be a number of reasons why people will look to the therapy. Clients may be looking for relaxation or to de-stress, they may need to sort out emotional problems, or maybe relieve or help sports injuries, or it may be just that they want to be pampered. It is your job to find out why they want to buy and whether you can deliver that.

For all therapies you need to be very clear what your customers demand, what competition is out there already and whether the market is growing or declining. Even if there is a large competition base there may be opportunities for joint ventures for example if you have complementary skills.

Why should customers buy from you? In other words what is your *unique selling proposition* (USP)? Unless you are clear why people should buy from you rather than anybody else then people may go to other businesses that are offering similar services or products.

Be aware that you may have indirect competition, where people are prepared to substitute different therapies to meet their needs (a different sort of therapy or massage for example).

Which niche to choose?

Research has shown that the more you specialize in your marketing the more effectively you can market to that group of people with very particular needs (known as a niche).

Firstly you need to look for your niche. For example an ex-student of mine specialised in rugby players because her partner was a rugby player, so she did further training and specialised in sports massage for rugby players. This obviously had implications for the quality of the massage table she needed, as a lot of the guys are 20 stone! The advantage was she would go to matches and could offer massage after the game, many of whom came to see her later in the week for a follow-up session. As rugby is seasonal, though, she had to find an additional niche for the summer months (she chose runners).

Another student liked the flexibility of being mobile (and had no room in her flat suitable for therapy) so she specialised in the niche of people who have mobility problems. It is unusual for psychotherapy to be done on a mobile basis as people often like the neutrality of the clinic situation, but certainly life coaching is often done over the phone (or by email) where this suits the customer better.

An ex-student commented that following her own difficult experiences, she decided to specialise in pregnancy and mothers in early years. In her first year after qualifying she struggled getting enough clients. When she specialized in pregnancy she attracted more than enough clients, for now she felt she could "really relate to them".

With the talking therapies and hypnotherapy it is not unusual to specialise in particular age groups or those with common issues for example quitting smoking, bereavement or relationships.

Asking round various therapist friends, people most often turn to therapy at major transitions in their lives. This can give you an opportunity to focus on one (or more niches). For example:
1.   marriage
2.   divorce
3.   redundancy
4.   retirement
5.   giving birth
6.   children leaving home
7.   bereavement

Alternatively, where people struggle in their lives:
1.   relationships
2.   finding a mate
3.   giving up smoking or drinking
4.   illness or pain
5.   weight issues
6.   self esteem and confidence

Who Pays the Piper?

You also need to be clear who will be paying for the treatment: is it the patient or client or the patient's parent, the NHS or a charity. Depending on who will pay you may need to target your marketing differently. You also need to determine how much they are prepared to pay and whether you will be able to make enough money to survive or thrive on. In **Module 7**, we will look at setting fees.

Market research: what is there already?

There are two sorts of market research:

Field research (primary) which covers performing face-to-face interviews of individuals or groups, telephone surveys, and postal or direct internet questionnaires.

Desk research (secondary) which covers research done by others on the Internet in trade magazines and newspapers, looking at industry surveys and reports or directories, some of which can be obtained from local libraries.

For field research the most effective type of research is face-to-face, which gives you an opportunity to talk to potential customers or focus groups. "Focus groups" is just a posh name for people getting together who have similar interests and ideally comprise people from your target market.

The market research should also give you the chance to look at what trends there are in the market, what opportunities there are for bridging a gap in needs and what potential threats there are too. Research should focus on the supply in the market already (competitors) and the demand from potential customers.

Step-by-Step Guide to Market Research

So how do you go about market research? You need to set up a database of potential customers and gather as much information as you can about them. You also need to determine your competitors.

Step 1: who else is out there?

The first step to finding out about your competitors is to:

1. look on the Internet
2. read alternative magazines
3. look in local newspapers and magazines
4. check the Yellow Pages
5. ask friends who they go to, who they would recommend, and why.

Step 2: compare and contrast

Set up a database of competitors (either on the computer or manually if you hate computers) and include the following information:

1. the range of services they offer
2. a cost per session
3. the ease of booking
4. their qualifications
5. their location
6. what is their pricing policy?
7. do they give concessions or block discounts?
8. particular specialisms they offer
9. how do they promote themselves?
10. how long have they been established?
11. who are their customers?
12. what are their values and business strategy (how do you think will they respond to a given set of circumstances)?
13. their strengths and weaknesses (this can be started now but is often completed after step 4—see below)
14. any further notes (for example, one person may be a well known therapist).

Step 3: gather your information while you may!

As an unknown individual, now is the time to glean as much information as possible. Therefore, for your five key competitors (those who are the most popular and successful):

1. look at their website, brochures and marketing material (it can give you ideas if nothing else!)
2. visit as many therapy rooms as you can
3. phone up and organise having a treatment.

Step 4: into the lion's den...

When you visit this is the perfect opportunity to be nosy! Some of the questions you can think about:

1. How are they set up and organised?
2. Are they close to where you intend to practise?
3. Have they positioned themselves in a similar niche to the one you have chosen?
4. Is it easy to find?
5. Is there parking/is it on a bus route?
6. What is the area like and is it appropriate for the way it is marketed (e.g. high end)?
7. Do they have a receptionist?
8. Does it seem professional?
9. Do they seem very busy?
10. How many different sorts of therapy are available?
11. What are the rooms like?
12. Is the clinic easily accessible?
13. How was the treatment/therapy?
14. What did you like/didn't like about the session?
15. Was it value for money?
16. Did they offer further sessions/additional services?
17. Would you recommend them, and if so, why?

Step 5 Assess your competitors strengths and weaknesses

Complete your assessment of the competition. What are their strengths and weaknesses?

Step 6 – work out your Unique Selling Proposition (USP)

This is perhaps the most crucial step and the one most people do not formalize or articulate. Decide and write down how you are going to differentiate your business from them. A word of warning: if you are planning just to give a low price service, you need to think about how your clients will think about you, how much harder you will need to work in order to make a living and how your competitors may react (they can probably sustain a lower price longer than you can).

If you cannot differentiate yourself from them then why should customers come to you rather than them? It isn't necessarily anything particularly earth-shattering.

An example—my USP

If it helps perhaps I could share my own USP (i.e. how I differentiate myself from my competitors). I am a life coach based near Bristol in the UK. If you search Google you will see there are some 285,000 results for "life coach Bristol". I do not advertise any longer, so how do I attract customers?

- I specialise in business coaching in the niche of therapists (obviously!);
- I have actually run my own businesses, which gives me credibility;
- I have additional professional qualifications (I am a chartered accountant);
- I have taught business on professional courses, at the local further education college and at degree level;
- I see clients face to face, or over the phone (actually Skype, although it does have a tendency to drop out at the crucial time!) or do email coaching (this is a growing trend I have noticed over the last year);
- I make an effort to be friendly and approachable, so people feel comfortable to ask me "stupid questions"... not that they *are* ever "stupid questions"!

An example of how your USP may look
Yours will obviously be different, but an example could be:

You are a massage therapist based in Birmingham in the UK. There are 348,000 hits on Google.

What is your specialism? Thai massage? Hawaiian? Sports? Aromatherapy? Swedish?

Do you have other qualifications which may be relevant? (nurses usually do quite well here as people trust them and assume that they know what they are doing)

Do you have other life or career experiences that will give you an understanding of potential clients (being a stressed parent could really help you to empathise with similar clients)?

What other activities do you do/could you do to help establish yourself as an "expert" (if you don't have anything yet, why not get involved in your therapy's governing body?);

How are you going to deliver the service? Maybe you will be joining a well-established clinic with a good reputation? Or can set up a very peaceful therapy room that can act as an "oasis" for your clients?

What are your personal attributes that will attract clients to you?

Market research – what is the demand?
Having decided which niche you are going to specialise in and having found out about your customers, you need to find out how big your market is and whether it is growing or declining and if you will need to change your niche, or location.

The UK National Government statistics Annual Business Inquiry shows that the category "physical well-being activities" has increased the number of registered entities from 374 in 1997 to 1,128 in 2007, a threefold increase. Turnover (sales) are shown as increasing 3.25 times in the same period. The category unfortunately is very broad, covering items as diverse as large city gyms to a small therapy clinic, so it is not possible to draw meaningful conclusions. It is worth stating though that there is an increase in demand for what is called "complementary and alternative medicine". Now that there is more regulation through the General Regulatory Council for Complementary Therapies (GRCCT) and the Complementary and Natural Healthcare Council (CNHC) the general public may feel more comfortable about seeing alternative therapists.

The Alliance and Leicester bank Bizguides state that

"Recent years have seen a huge increase in, and use of, complementary and alternative medicine (CAM), for a number of reasons:
- *GPs have little time to devote to their patients*
- *conventional healthcare has become more impersonal*
- *patients are concerned about the increasing use of powerful drugs*
- *many conditions such as asthma, arthritis or back pain do not respond satisfactorily to conventional treatment*
- *patients are better informed and more willing to try alternative therapies*
- *complementary therapists are providing an increasingly professional service*
- *the medical profession has acknowledged the benefit to patients of providing both conventional and complementary treatment*
- *the number of complementary therapists has grown, so that people can more easily access them"*

Desk research
For desk research on the size of the market you can:

1. search the internet (see below)
2. read market intelligence reports (these tend to be expensive but can usually be accessed for free at business libraries)
3. consult local chambers of commerce
4. consult trade journals and magazines
5. attend exhibitions
6. obtain published accounts of your competitors from http://www. companieshouse.gov.uk/

Unfortunately most therapists are not incorporated into companies (see **Module 3**) so the accounts information will not exist from Companies House. If accounts are available you can see whether your competitors are profitable or not. If they are not that is that an indicator that there may not be sufficient demand in the area, or, conversely, they have weaknesses of which you may be able to take opportunity.

Useful Internet sites:

It is definitely worth looking at the bizguides as they have useful information and links for most therapies:
https://www.alliance-leicestercommercialbank.co.uk/bizguides/full/index.asp

Looking at the market size and market potential again it is worth looking at the Internet on websites such as the following which show the demographic by particular postcode
http://www.upmystreet.com
http://www.caci.com
and sometimes Business Link do regional statistics that can be helpful:
http://www.businesslink.co.uk

To check market trends it is worth looking at the websites of the governing bodies of your particular therapy, finding out the number of registrations and perhaps even talking to some of the officials on the various councils.

For market information and reports other websites to look at are:
http://www.keynote.co.uk
http://www.snapdata.com/index.php?module=search
http://uk.nielsen.com/site/index.shtml
http://reports.mintel.com/
All of these are expensive to access but can be viewed via business libraries (often at universities).

Field research

Field research is when you gather data yourself. This can be done in a number of different ways:

1. Local surveys (see below for guidelines)

If you are planning to set up in a certain locality you can do a questionnaire or survey. Generally response rates for questionnaires and surveys are very low (ten per cent is good) unless people feel that they are making a real contribution.

2. Online surveys

It is possible to do surveys online using websites such as http://www.surveymonkey.com/

3. Interviews of experts

It is worth interviewing colleagues and ex-tutors to find out how they set up in business what they would suggest to do to help set-up, what they think the available market is in that area that you wish to specialise in.

4. Interview potential customers and suppliers

5. Doing talks

This can also give you an opportunity to discuss with people face to face what their needs are as well as marketing your services.

6. Telephone surveys

Phoning up people to ask whether they are interested in your services, although be careful as a lot of people do not one want to be interrupted at home. Also what they say is not necessarily what they do!

7. Ask distributors their professional opinion about the market

For example the supplier of aromatherapy oils or massage couch paper will be able to tell you whether they are getting more or less orders.

8. Ask training schools how many people they have on their courses

How many courses are run locally and what percentage of students find jobs or set up in business after they have trained?

9. Test the service to find out the reaction

You can distribute fliers if you are offering a service locally. Sometimes it can be useful to "split test" the fliers: one perhaps that offering a discount another offering a reduced service or maybe giveaways such as an aromatherapy oil and see the take up.

Try to replicate your target market in your field research.

Obviously if you are doing your own field research you need to ensure you have a representative sample. For example, if you are targeting stressed housewives who have children and not much time there is not much point in doing a survey in the shopping malls around the time when they have to pick up children from school. If you want to obtain a more broad-based sample of the population you will need to ensure that you cover different areas, different times of day, different interest groupings.

Tips for Compiling Questionnaires

If you are compiling a questionnaire it must be:

1.   structured so it is simple and easy to follow

2. preferably no more than one page long
3. impartial—does not "lead" the respondent to give you the answers you desire.

A ten per cent response rate for questionnaire is considered to be a good response. Again, in choosing whether to go for a postal questionnaire, face to face survey or Internet questionnaire you need to consider your target market. Young people are unlikely to respond to a postal questionnaire and the retired target markets are less likely to be comfortable with an Internet questionnaire.

An example of a questionnaire is given on **page 31**.

Interviewing experts

Another really valuable resource is to actually interview somebody who is already in a similar or the same business that you want to go into. Try and make it flow naturally as a conversation and keep your questions to a maximum of ten.

A list of questions to ask them could include:
1. Tell me a little bit about yourself and your background
2. What made you go into this particular service or therapy
3. What was your prior experience and what skills did you have for your particular business?
4. What methods did you use to source funding to set up the organisation?
5. What were the biggest challenges setting up the organisation?
6. What are the biggest challenges you face now in running the organisation?
7. What are the measures of success of your enterprise?
8. What are your future plans for the enterprise?
9. What are the risks faced by your enterprise?
10. What advice would you give someone setting up in this business?

Questionnaire

It is really important that your target questionnaire focuses on the same population of those that you want to include in your niche.

In your questionnaire you can ask closed questions (i.e., those that give you a yes or no answer) and open questions (those that require more consideration and a more full response).

As a general rule it is easier to analyse closed questions numerically, but often the open questions provide the most interesting answers! Therefore it is useful to have a balance of both closed and open questions in your questionnaire.

Ten Tips for a Questionnaire

1. Do not use leading questions (that is, anticipating an answer from your respondent). To get around this it is often easier to use multiple-choice answers.
2. Do not use jargon or difficult words.
3. Do not ask two questions in one sentence as this can be confusing and you rarely get an answer to both parts of the question. Restructure the two parts into two separate questions.
4. Give an introduction to what you are going to be doing and how long it is going to take.
5. Ask a maximum of ten to twelve questions.
6. Be very clear why you are asking each question and what you want to achieve with the answers.
7. Time your questionnaire intelligently—if your target market are busy mothers an easier time to ask questions is during the morning when they're at the shops rather than when they are rushing to collect their children from school. Try different places that they may go, for example to the mall or the leisure centre, or perhaps while waiting for the schoolchildren to come out of school.
8. Choose the method of survey to match the needs of your target market. Using the busy mums example asking for a telephone

survey at a time when they are busy cooking tea and on a deadline to pick up children from various activities is not a good time. Personally I hate telephone surveys and I have never done one, but I do understand that they are invaluable for accessing those people who do not normally have time to go to public places.

9.   Make sure your questionnaire asks exactly the questions that you need. There is no point constructing a questionnaire that doesn't provide the answers you want. It is worth spending a bit of time testing it on friends before trying it on the general public.

10.   Be sure to thank the people for their time, and give out a business card or leaflet that has your contact details on.

One great technique I have seen used to entice people to complete the questionnaire is to offer a prize draw for which they had to give their contact details. A free course of sessions is the main prize but you also have a willing market who can be offered "runner-up" prizes of a free session to see how they get on and you have their contact details so you can email them later on and start to build a relationship with them.

Bonus tip!

If you have done the market research, don't ignore it! I have come across a number of people who, having found out that something wouldn't work, refused to alter their plans. They persisted because they had set their hearts on it—only for it to fail a year and a half later because they ignored the market research information that they had.

An example questionnaire

1   Which therapies have you received in the last year?
  a) psychotherapy or counselling
  b) massage—aromatherapy, Swedish or sports massage
  c) reflexology
  d) acupuncture
  e) chiropractor or osteopathy

f) Reiki
g) hypnotherapy
h) other—please specify _____
i) none

2   **What did you hope to achieve by using that therapy?**
a) de-stress
b) dealing with an emotional or psychological problem or issue
c) dealing with trauma
d) relaxation or pleasure
e) dealing with physical injury
f) stop smoking or drinking, for example
g) other—please specify _____

3   **Did it succeed? If not, what more would you have liked?**

4   **What type of therapy do you prefer and why?**

5   **Would you be prepared to try [your therapy] with a half-price introductory session?**

6   **How much would you be prepared to pay for the therapy session?**
a) less than £20 for a half-hour session
b) between £20 and £35 for a half-hour session
c) between £35 and £45 for a half-hour session
d) more than £45 for a half-hour session

7   **What time of day would you prefer to have therapy?**
a) early morning
b) late morning
c) early afternoon
d) late afternoon
e) early evening
f) late evening

8   How often do you go to a therapist?
   a) once a week
   b) once a fortnight
   c) once a month
   d) less than once a month

9   How far are you prepared to go to see a therapist?
   a) less than 1 mile
   b) between one and 2 miles
   c) more than 2 miles

10   What is your age?
   a) less than 30
   b) 30 to 50
   c) 50+

11   If you would like to be entered the prize drawn for extra free sessions please leave your contact details, name and telephone number and email address

Obviously if someone says that they don't believe in alternative therapies there's no point continuing with the questionnaire as they are unlikely be a future customer!

Analysing the results

You can analyse the results with charts, tables, pie charts, etc. Examples are shown at the end for the questionnaire shown above done on surveymonkey.com (which is free unless you want to download the results). This is done with a small poll of my friends so isn't indicative of your market for therapies! I imported the summary information into Excel and charted the results. Included are a few of the interesting results.

Chart 1 (overleaf) is the list of therapies that my friends had used in the last year. I was surprised that none had gone to reflexology or hypnotherapy:

Chart 1: Therapies used in the last year

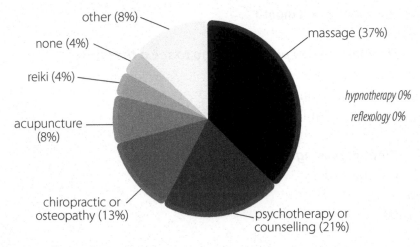

Below are their reasons for going to therapy. Note that almost two-thirds (65%) went to de-stress, for pleasure or relaxation!

Chart 2: Reason for going to therapy

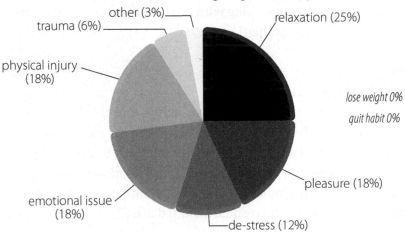

It is interesting to note their price preference: over half would spend more than £35 per hour. Now of course this is not a reflection of the population as a whole, however if you target your market research well you should get a clear steer on what they state they are prepared to pay. You might want to probe more deeply: are the people who wished to deal with injuries, for instance, prepared to pay more? (This is certainly what I found from various pieces of research I have done.)

Chart 3: Price preference (one-hour session)

up to £25 (8%)

£46 to £60 (15%)

over £60 0%

£36 to £45 (38%)

£26 to £35 (39%)

The following chart shows a result I had not expected: how far people are prepared to travel. One respondent commented she travelled to a different country to see her therapist! Now *that* is customer loyalty!

Chart 4: Distance prepared to travel

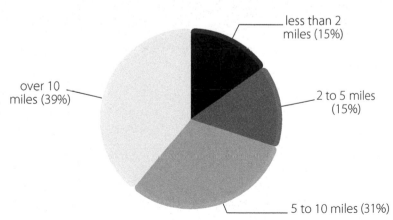

less than 2 miles (15%)

over 10 miles (39%)

2 to 5 miles (15%)

5 to 10 miles (31%)

Summary

Market research is critical if you want to have a successful business, to find out if there is a market for your service and what the competition is already. Even if you find it confirms what you already know, that is reassurance!

So, assuming that the market research has shown that there is a marketplace for your niche, your next step is to decide which legal form you wish to trade under. Let's go on to **Module 3: What Shape Should you Take?**

Module 3:
What Shape Should you Take?
Legal Form

One of the key decisions you need to make at the beginning of setting up a business is the legal form that you will take. Although they are relatively easy to set up, changing later on can be quite expensive, therefore it is worthwhile thinking about what you need, and what is appropriate for what you want.

The three main types of business data status are **sole trader**, **partnership** or **limited company**. If you are going into business on your own you can be either a sole trader or limited company. If you are going into business with others you can have:
- a general partnership,
- a limited liability partnership,
- a limited company, or
- a cooperative.

The features of a Sole Trader

Advantages:
1. It is easy to set up: register for self-employed tax and national insurance with Her Majesty's Revenue and Customs (or tax authorities in your country).
2. All profits belong to the owner.

3. You make all the decisions of the business.
4. There are no strict rules of keeping accounts. Details of income and expenditure including receipts must be kept for six years. For tax purposes, you must keep "proper books and records". In **Module 12** I'll cover what you will need to keep as a minimum.
5. Taxes are paid on the net business profits (I will explain what this means in **Module 12** and **Module 13**) before taking the owner's salary (called "drawings").
6. Business losses can be offset against tax on other sources of income in the year.
7. Class 2 National Insurance is payable at a fixed rate and Class 4 National Insurance is also payable on the profits when tax is paid. This will be discussed later on in **Module 13** about tax and National Insurance.

Disadvantages:

1. The big disadvantage of a sole trader is that there is unlimited liability—that means you are *personally* responsible for all business debts, and the creditors can come after your personal assets if the business gets into trouble.
2. The other disadvantage of a sole trader is that it is often more difficult to secure funds.

The features of a General Partnership

Advantages:

1. It is also easy to set up, the partnership is registered with Her Majesty's Revenue and Customs for income tax and national insurance.
2. Profits are shared by the partners, as are losses!
3. Partners share responsibility for business decisions (which can also be a disadvantage – see below).
4. Accounts preparation is again relatively simple and there is no requirement to file them with any authorities.

5. A partnership tax return is completed each year that shows the partnership profits and tax due for each individual partner. Each individual partner then includes their share of the profits or losses in their own personal tax return. See the section on taxation in **Module 13**.
6. If you choose your partner well, you can have complementary skills and preferences that can make life a lot easier!

Disadvantages:

1. Like a sole trader in a general partnership, the partners also have unlimited liability. In the case of the partnership, you are liable for both your own and your partner's business debts.
2. A further disadvantage is that it is more difficult to get funds for a partnership.
3. For a general partnership, when one partner leaves the partnership, the partnership is technically disbanded and recommenced, even though it may continue trading. This has implications for tax purposes.
4. As you can see from the above, there are even bigger risks being involved with other people in a partnership.

One of my clients had a business partnership with someone who had been her best friend. Unfortunately the business partner became ill when she was pregnant and couldn't work, but still expected to get 50% of the profits. This caused a rift between the partners—and further, when the taxman came and demanded a large sum of money, the partner who had been ill said she could not pay, so my client had to pay both her share of taxes and that of her partner. This was sufficient to push the partnership out of business, and perhaps more crucially for them, caused the breakdown of their friendship.

If you are going to go into business with other people it is absolutely critical to have a **partnership agreement**. A partnership agreement should set out what happens in different scenarios, clarifying roles and responsibilities, specifying profit share and share of losses, what the procedure is in the event of a major disagreement, and how the partnership will operate on a day-to-day basis.

The features of a Limited Liability Partnership

A limited liability partnership was introduced in the UK as a halfway house between a general partnership and a company. That is, a limited liability partnership does not get disbanded in the event of one partner leaving, and each partner has limited liability. What that means is the partner is only liable to the extent that they have invested in the business. In short, the limited liability partnership is a legal entity, it can sue and be sued in its own name in a way similar to a company. The big difference is that the partners are still taxed as individuals through their own self-assessment tax returns. A limited liability partnership also needs to:

- be registered with the Registrar of Companies,
- complete an annual return which is sent to Companies House each year with a fee, and
- complete an annual tax return, which is sent to Her Majesty's Revenue and Customs.

If you do not "incorporate" (do business through a company) and are in business with someone else, I recommend using a limited liability partnership. You will still need a partnership agreement.

The features of a Limited Company

A company is owned by shareholders, who invest in shares in the company. The shareholders receive dividends (income) from their investment in the company. The directors are employees of the company and run the company on a day-to-day basis.

Advantages:

1. A company is relatively easy to set up, although more formal documents need to be drawn up and maintained, and the company needs to be registered with the Registrar of Companies.

2.   Profits are paid out to shareholders, who are the owners of the business, by way of dividends. The owners of the business (the shareholders) can be separate from the people who run the business (the directors).

3.   The board of directors controls the business on a day-to-day basis. The shareholders can focus on certain issues at the annual general meeting including, for example, appointing or removing directors, agreeing directors' pay, agreeing to the appointment of auditors, agreeing to payment of dividends and agreeing a change in share capital.

4.   A company has limited liability, and has a legal identity so can sue or be sued.

5.   It is usually easier to sell on shares in a company (or issue new shares for a new investor coming into the business).

6.   It is usually easier for a company to obtain funding. However a word of warning: banks will often require a personal guarantee secured on the owner's house. Thus in the event of the business collapsing, the bank will call in that guarantee and the owner could still lose their house, despite owning a company that has limited liability!

Disadvantages:

1.   The directors are employees of the company, and a payroll needs to be run for them. Their income tax is payable via pay as you earn (PAYE) on their salary. All employees pay Class 1 National Insurance, and the employer also pays National Insurance contributions. National Insurance will be discussed further in **Module 13**. The profits of the company are subject to corporation tax.

2.   There are much stricter controls on accounting and the accounts, in a particular format, need to be filed with Companies House each year. Large companies need to have their accounts audited by independent auditors. An annual return needs to be completed and sent to Companies House each year with a fee. All of these increase the cost of running a business.

The usual form for therapists

Of course the critical thing is to determine which business form is easiest to you. I did a quick survey locally and for businesses listed in the Yellow Pages under complementary therapies, 60% were sole traders, 34% were partnerships or clinics (where you can't tell which is which). Interestingly only 5% were companies (and all but one of these were shops or suppliers). The remaining 1% were colleges. Why such a high percentage of sole traders? Well, therapy, unlike most businesses, focuses on the individual who is providing this service. People have a loyalty to particular therapists. There may also be an element that people want to keep below the VAT income threshold (for details see the HMRC website, http://www.hmrc.gov.uk/vat/forms-rates/rates/rates-thresholds.htm), as most of their clients will be individuals who cannot reclaim VAT, rather than registered businesses, which can.

Clinics can be run as companies, although this is unusual unless it is something like a leisure centre or spa. Most clinics are run as a partnership, or even as sole traders who rent rooms to other therapists.

I have assumed in the rest of this that you are either a sole trader or partnership, rather than a company. With this in mind it is probably easier to set up in the first place as a sole trader.

10 Steps to Set Up as a Sole Trader

Setting up as a sole trader is very simple:

1. Register for Tax and National Insurance: Contact Her Majesty's Revenue and Customs and register as self-employed. See Revenue and Customs Business Startup: http://www.hmrc.gov.uk/startingup/index.htm

2. Decide on a business name: There is a register of business names, however it is not mandatory to register your business names with this organisation, and this does not guarantee that no-one else will use the name. If you use a business name which is different from your own, you will need to include your personal name on all of your stationery and for bank accounts will need to declare that you are "your name" trading as "the business name".

In terms of choosing a name that is not your own it helps to have something that is:

- easy to spell (be careful using numbers as people are never sure whether to spell them in full or write the number)
- easy to remember
- has a website available
- describes what you do ("does what it says on the tin"), and
- ideally it will also describe how you are differentiated from your competition

3. Comply with Regulations: Ensure you have complied with all regulations and obtained the relevant insurances (see **Module 4**).

4. Write a Business Plan (see **Module 5**).

5. Set up a Bank Account: I am often asked if you need a separate account. It is good practice and makes it easier to keep your business expenses away from your personal expenses (and the tax authorities recommend that you do).

 Most big banks will give out lots of information to help small businesses. Go around and ask questions and pick up as much information as possible. Business bank accounts are usually not free. An exception is the Alliance+Leicester and some internet branches of high street banks. Triodos and Co-operative have a good ethical reputation, but check that they are not more expensive than the competition, and the ease of access to the branch network.

6. Devise a Marketing Plan: This is not just about putting up a couple of adverts in your local newsagents and inserts in the local paper. See **Module 10**.

7. Equip your Business: Ensure that you have the appropriate equipment. If you are going to act as your own receptionist don't forget you will need to have an answering machine!

8. Begin Marketing: See **Module 10** and **Module 11**.

9. Set up your Books and Accounts: Module 12 will cover this.

10. Start Work...

More resources
There are many resources that will help to decide on your legal form, and to help you set up in business, although none of them focus on therapy businesses.

For a general introduction I recommend
- Business link: http://www.businesslink.gov.uk/
- Brochures from banks.

Summary
Most therapists start up as a sole trader (or in partnership) although there are risks with limited liability. Most clients are loyal to one therapist so this legal form can be an advantage rather than a disadvantage. From here on I will assume that you are set up either as a sole trader or partnership.

Module 4: Licence to Heal

The Regulations and
Insurances you need

•
•
•
●

Below are some of the insurances that you need to consider when setting up in business as a therapist:

1. Car Insurance
It is mandatory to have third-party insurance if you drive a car. If you use it for business then you will need to notify your insurer and pay the additional premium. That insurance will be allowable against your taxes, which will be covered in **Module 13.**

2. Professional Indemnity Insurance, including Malpractice Insurance
This is usually a requirement of the governing body for your particular therapy. You can usually get a reduced premium through organisations such as the Federation of Holistic Therapists. Check your regulatory body.

3. Selling-on Products
This can usually be added onto your professional indemnity insurance.

4. Public Liability Insurance of your place of work
If you have people coming to your place of work (including your home) you need to take out public liability insurance in the event that they trip and injure themselves, for example. When you work in a clinic you

will need to check that their public liability insurance will cover you working in that clinic. As part of the conditions of rental some clinics will actually allocate part of their cost of insurance for public liability onto you. You will need to check the details of the contract very carefully (see **Module 6**).

5. Employers' Liability Insurance

This is required by law if you employ staff.

6. Property Insurance, including contents

If you are running a business from home you will need to notify your insurer and pay the additional premium for buildings and contents insurance and also for the additional security risk. Again as part of the clinic you will need to find out from the contract whether they will cover your equipment under their insurance or if you are expected to take out your own insurance.

7. Legal Expenses Insurance

This is often included as an add-on to professional indemnity insurance. It covers you if you have to go to court or to a solicitor, and in litigation some of your legal expenses may be covered. It is worthwhile checking what is excluded from the legal expenses insurance if you decide to go for this.

8. Critical Illness Insurance

This insurance covers the position where you are unable to work due to illness or injury. It is worth checking the exclusions from the policy, for example the length of time you are ill or the types of injuries that would not be covered.

9. Business Disruption Insurance

This insurance is payable in the event that you cannot run your business following a fire or flood to the premises. You would need to check the premiums payable and weigh that up against the possibility of being able to find contingency in the event of a disruption. For example, you may be able to rent rooms in a local clinic.

10. Tax Investigation Insurance

This is a relatively new insurance that some firms of accountants offer. This is to cover the accountancy fees in the event of an investigation by Her Majesty's Revenue and Customs. It does not cover the cost of any additional tax or penalties. If you set up a business correctly in the early years it is unlikely that you would have a tax investigation (unless you are being fraudulent, of course!) as your profits are likely to be low and therefore not worth being investigated by the tax inspectors.

Obviously there are some insurances that are mandatory; for others you will need to decide whether you go ahead, depending on the risk of recurrence and the implications of that risk.

Regulations

Health and Safety Regulations

The Health and Safety Executive (HSE) is responsible for ensuring the health and safety laws are maintained by all businesses within the UK. A local authority inspector can make unscheduled visitors to the therapist's premises. If any problems are discovered in their visit an initial improvement notice will be issued and changes will need to be made within the next few weeks, which will be checked again on a return visit. In the event that the changes have not been made a prohibition notice will be issued and/or business activity must be stopped until the problems have been resolved. In reality this is a very rare occurrence, particularly where a therapist is doing business in a professional manner and has a professional setup.

The Health and Safety at Work Act 1974 (HSWA) is the key act relating to public health and safety. The HSWA states that business owners must ensure that any clients or self-employed workers who are hiring rooms, or other visitors, are not exposed to any risks to their health and safety whilst on the premises. Later acts specify what the responsibilities of the business owner are.

Risk Assessment

By law a business owner should carry out a risk assessment, to establish and implement procedures to protect the health and wellbeing of all visitors to their premises and to prevent accidents:

- Ensure that there is one or more competent person appointed to implement the procedures. This normally includes first aid. In some therapies it is a requirement of training that a first aid certificate is attained. It will be necessary to keep this current.
- Perform a regular check to ensure health and safety is being carried out, and keep a record of those checks. See **"Health and Safety: Risk Assessment"** on page 54.
- An accident book needs to be maintained and reportable accidents or diseases included therein.

Workplace and Equipment Regulations

The Workplace (Health, Safety and Welfare) Regulations 1992 cover the appearance of all parts of the premises, not just the treatment rooms. To meet the regulations the premises must:

1. be clean and tidy, including all staff and client toilets, with hot and cold running water and adequate soap and towels and/or hand dryers;
2. be well ventilated from windows with clean air-conditioning;
3. be well lit in all areas with the ability to control lighting, for example lights may be dimmed during treatments;
4. be maintained at a comfortable temperature of at least 16°C, although this may be warmer if clients are expected to remove clothing;
5. be clear of all waste material;
6. have a fire extinguisher available which should be easily accessible and stored complete with instructions for use;
7. be supplied with drinking water;

8.   have floors and traffic routes free from obstructions.

Other regulations cover the use of equipment and electrical equipment. In short equipment, should be suitable for use and properly maintained. A qualified electrician should check electrical equipment annually.

Fire Regulations

The Regulatory Reform (Fire Safety) Order 2005 requires a "responsible person"—you—to carry out, implement and maintain a five-step fire safety risk assessment. The steps you will need to go through to carry out a fire risk assessment within your premises are:

Step 1 - Identify fire hazards
- Sources of ignition
- Sources of fuel

Step 2 - Identify people especially at risk
- Members of staff
- People not familiar with the premises
- People working alone

Step 3 - Evaluate, remove, reduce and protect from risks
- Measures to prevent fires
- Measures to protect people from fire

Step 4 - Record, plan, instruct, inform and train
- Record significant findings and actions taken
- Prepare an emergency plan
- Inform relevant people, provide instruction, co-operate and co-ordinate with others
- Provide training

Step 5 - Review
- Keep assessment under review
- Revise where necessary

Your local fire safety officer can advise on fire issues, including whether a fire certificate is necessary. See http://www.fire.gov.uk

Hazardous Substances

Control of Substances Hazardous to Health Act 1989 ("COSHH") provides guidance on dealing with chemical substances that could cause skin irritation, allergies and burns and potentially cause difficulties in breathing or could be life-threatening. It covers the handling and storage of hazardous substances and the disposal of such substances. Some essential oils are considered to be hazardous to health, thus if you are an aromatherapist you will need to know how to deal with such substances.

First Aid

The Health and Safety (First Aid) Regulations 1981 cover the event of an injury. This means:
1.   there is a qualified first aider who is regularly available;
2.   a fully stocked first aid box should be available, which also contains guidance on how to treat injuries;
3.   notices are displayed providing information about the location of the first aid box and who is responsible for the first aid.

Reporting Requirements

The Reporting of Injuries Diseases and Dangerous Occurrences Regulations 1995 ("RIDDOR") outline the correct procedure to adopt if an accident occurs in the workplace. Businesses need to:
1.   have an accident book;
2.   ensure any injury or dangerous occurrence is written in the accident book immediately after it happens with as many details as possible;
3.   report accidents to the local authority immediately by telephone, and follow up with a written report within 10 days, if the event involves death, poisoning, electric shock or major injury;
4.   act appropriately in the situation, making the injured and the premises safe; and
5.   keep records of all incidents for at least three years.

Other Health and Safety regulations

Further details of all regulations relating to health and safety can be found at the HSE website. Major considerations are those around protecting yourself (and staff if you have them) including handling equipment, posture, taking breaks etc. Most of this should have been covered in your therapy training. Check the HSE website: http://www.hse.gov.uk

Local Authority Bylaws: Acupuncture

Where therapists practice invasive treatments on the premises, for example tattooing or acupuncture, they are required to register and be licensed by the local authority's environmental health department. An environmental health officer will make unscheduled visits to the premises to ensure that:

1. all equipment is thoroughly clean and sterilised;
2. only fully-qualified therapists are employed in practice;
3. waste products are appropriately disposed of in a safe and hygienic way;
4. the premises are kept meticulously clean; and
5. the certificate of registration is displayed.

Local Authority Bylaws: Massage

Certain local authorities require a license in order to practice massage; or massage might only be carried out between certain hours. You may need to contact your local authority or visit their website which can be found via http://local.direct.gov.uk/LDGRedirect/Start.do?mode=1

Planning Permission

If you alter the premises you may need planning permission. Again, this will depend on your local authority.

Business Rates

The occupier of a non-domestic property pays business rates. If a separate building, for example a garage, is converted for business use, or a large percentage of the house is used for business purposes, you may need to apply to the local council to apply for change of use and pay business rates. Also if you subsequently sell your house, the non-domestic part is not eligible for the exemption from capital gains tax on your main home.

Data Protection Act

Where details are held about individuals and are used for advertising, public relations or marketing or for accounts and records you will be required to notify the Information Commissioner's Office under the Data Protection Act. Notification can be done by fax or email and costs £35 per annum. See http://www.ico.gov.uk/what_we_cover/data_protection/notification.aspx

Disability Discrimination Act

The Disability Discrimination Act (DDA) gives disabled people important rights of access to everyday services that include therapies, and places such as clinics.

This service is not just about installing ramps and widening doorways for wheelchair users—it is about making services easier to use for all disabled people, including people who are blind, deaf or have a learning disability. More details can be obtained from http://www.direct.gov.uk under "disabled people."

Under the Disability Discrimination Act it is against the law for service providers to treat disabled people less favourably than other people through reason of their disability. Service providers need to make reasonable adjustments to the way they deliver their services so that disabled people can use them. Examples include providing an induction loop for people who use hearing aids; larger, well-defined signage for people with impaired vision; or a ramp at the entrance to the building instead of steps. What is considered to be reasonable adjustment for a large organisation will be different from a reasonable adjustment for a small business. You will not be required to make changes that are impractical or beyond your financial means.

There is a PDF document, published by the Disability Rights Commission (now the Equality and Human Rights Commission), called *Making Access To Goods And Services Easier For Disabled Customers*. It is available to download at http://www.direct.gov.uk/prod_consum_dg/groups/dg_digitalassets/@dg/@en/documents/digitalasset/dg_070741.pdf

For small businesses such as therapies the emphasis is on practical, low-cost adjustments, although you should consider other major physical alterations if it is feasible and affordable. Examples of adjustments that can be made are:

1. Any signs and written documents being in large print to help those with impaired vision. When we owned a therapy school we had one student who was partially-sighted and we got all of the handouts made in large print.
2. If adjustments are to be made to the premises it is worthwhile considering putting in ramps, an accessible toilet, and having doors wide enough to allow wheelchairs to enter.
3. Some massage therapists and other physical therapists will provide a mobile service for their disabled clients, whereby they go to the disabled person's house to provide the appropriate treatment.

Does that mean you will be put out of business if you do not have an accessible toilet and ramp, for example? No, but you should not discriminate against people on the grounds of disability and you should be able to demonstrate that you have taken appropriate, practical steps to accommodate disabled clients.

Phonographic Performance Limited

If you play music in your clinic you will need to obtain a licence to play music. Information can be obtained from http://www.prsformusic.com or http://www.ppluk.com/en/Music-Users/Playing-Music-and-Videos-In-Public/

Health and Safety: Risk Assessment

The Health And Safety Executive produces a number of booklets about health and safety for businesses. You can obtain a health and safety "starter pack" from the HSE for £35 (although most of the guides are available individually from the HSE website if you are prepared to sit there and download them!) Check http://www.hse.gov.uk/business.pack.htm

For businesses that have five or more employees you should have a health and safety policy. Again an example is available from the HSE website. Even if you are self-employed, it is worthwhile looking at the first page that shows which areas will be covered, but obviously the parts that relate to apportioning responsibility will not be necessary as you will be responsible for all of them!

The law requires that you carry out a risk assessment to help assess your health and safety risks. Templates are available from the HSE website.

A risk assessment is a careful examination of what in your work could cause harm to people, so that you can weigh up whether you have taken sufficient precautions or should do more to prevent harm. Workers and visitors have the right to be protected from harm caused by your failure to take reasonable control measures. You are legally required to assess the risks in your workplace so you can put into place a plan to control the risks.

How to assess the risks in your workplace

1. Identify the hazards
2. Decide who might be harmed and how. [I also tend to do a calculation showing the probability of that instance occurring and the impact if that risk occurred. So for example I might say that there is a low risk of fire happening but there would be high impact. If I apportion a number of 1 to low risk and 3 to high risk or high

impact to assess a risk rating, I would multiply the risk factor by the impact factor. In this case the risk rating would be 3. For a computer virus the likelihood might be medium (because I have a Mac rather than a PC, which would probably be high risk!) and the impact would also be medium as it would impair my ability to proceed with business as usual. Thus the risk factor will be to multiply 2×2, i.e., 4.]

3. Evaluate the risks and decide on precautionary measures and contingencies
4. Record your findings and implement them
5. Review your assessment on a regular basis and update if necessary.

Available as a download from my website is an example of a risk assessment for a massage therapy clinic. Obviously it is general in nature, but it may give you an idea of how to complete it.

Summary

In order to set up you need to be aware of a number of regulations. Most of the health and safety regulations are "common sense" including performing a risk assessment as required by law. Local authorities will need to be contacted to find out about licences, rates etc.

Once you have all that sorted you are ready to prepare your business plan. Are you ready? Let's go…

Module 5:
A Cunning Little Plan
Business Planning

Most business books, websites and banks will tell you that you need to have a business plan. You can pick up templates of business plans from banks and download them from the Internet on various sites such as Business Link and the Small Business Administration in the United States. You can find a template that is relevant for a therapy business; however, it is really important that you actually go through the thinking process itself.

What is a business plan?

A business plan is a way of setting out the goals and objectives for your business in the medium to longer term (up to about five years). A good business plan will include not just financial projections (which we will cover in **Module 12**), but also:

- who is running the business, and what skills and weaknesses they have,
- what and where the business is,
- who will buy from the business,
- how big the market is for the business,
- what the risks are to the business, both in terms of income streams and costs,
- what the opportunities are for growth,
- how you will get funding to cover the period until the business is established,

- who the competitors are, their strengths and weaknesses,
- how you will achieve success. This covers the detailed steps needed to set up (milestone planning) and also your measures of success. The latter can cover when you start breaking even, payback period, and also "softer" measures of success—which could be treating a certain number of people within the first year, obtaining a satisfactory-or-better rating from all of your customers, or other such measures that you wish to achieve.

Why do you need a business plan?

If you ask most people they will say it is so that you can show outside investors that you are a "safe bet" and they should invest in you. If you have ever seen the BBC programme *Dragon's Den*, in essence what the business people are presenting is a very short version of their business plan, with the idea of getting investors and mentors to help them. If you haven't watched it I strongly recommend it, as it is interesting to see how they are challenged and how they are caught out if they have not thought through their business idea.

The business plan should really be for the owners of the business: to make sure that you have thought through all the various aspects and whether you have the skills to be in business; to determine whether the business plan is workable and whether you have a feasible business. It is also crucial for the cash flow forecast to have something to measure against and control your business against as you go along and if necessary take avoiding action, i.e., reducing your salary (called "drawings"), increasing your sales effort, or reducing costs. Cash flow forecasts will be covered in **Module 12**.

Contents Of A Business Plan

Cover Page: name of business, address and contact details

Index/Contents if it is a long business plan

Section 1: Executive Summary

I always complete this section last, as it is literally a summary of the key points in the body of the text. The purpose of the executive summary is to ensure that the reader, who may be a potential investor, understands about the business and knows your unique selling proposition (USP). In short the USP is the answer to the question why people should buy from you rather than anyone else, or what makes your business special and different. Until you can answer that question you need to go back and determine that, before investing more time and funds into your business. Just to reiterate the point it is important that you complete the plan as you know your service and the market better than anyone else. You can get advice in writing the plan: Business Link do various training courses, and accountants are happy to help... for a fee!

1.1 **Description of business:**

You need to give a brief description of the business, including your unique selling point and your niche target market

1.2 **Finance required:**

You need to state what finance you are requesting from investors and what you are going to use it for.

The main types of finance are:

a. for a company to issue shares to investors who will have some rights in the company and be entitled to share in the ongoing profit but also take some of the risks; this will not apply to most therapists as they do not set up as a company

b. to obtain a bank loan. Banks do not share in the risks of the business, nor do they benefit from any increase in profit or suffer from any losses. They will charge a rate of interest on the loan outstanding, and demand repayment over a period of time. Interest on a business loan is allowable against tax but it also means it has to be paid out before any profits are distributed to the owners of the business. If a therapist has a business loan from a bank the interest and capital (loan) re-payments will need to be included in the cash flow forecasts.

c. to obtain a loan from friends and family. This is often the easiest form of funding to be obtained but can cause the greatest issues if anything goes wrong or if the investor feels they have a right to tell you how to run your business.

1.3 Financial projections

Key highlights for profit and the payback period and breakeven should be included. Ideally figures should be for the next three to five years.

1.4 Business differentiators

What makes the business different from the competition? In essence this is your USP. Your USP does not necessarily need to be anything too technical: it might be you are the only counsellor or psychotherapist in your area of town specialising in teenagers, for example.

1.5 Business credibility

In essence, this should be about who you are. What are your qualifications, your track record, your skills, etc. Do you have a list of the skills and specialities of other key people in your team even if they do not work for you full-time, for example, do you have a business mentor or bookkeeper?

1.6 Prospects for the investor/lender

The lender will need to know when they're going to get their money back with interest. As a sole trader therapist you will need to show to the bank when you will have repaid the loan and also that you have the funds to cover the interest throughout the loan period. Even if you have a loan from friends or family it is still useful for them to know when you consider you will be able to refund the money to them with any interest that you have agreed. Research shows that people who have lent money to somebody, remember very clearly when they are due for that money to be returned. Therefore, make sure that you give yourself enough time to pay back the loan.

Section 2: Purpose of the business

The purpose of this section is to set out your values and objectives for the business, your key "competencies" and if you have started already in the business, your results to date. You also need to give some idea the market trends that you anticipate over the next three years. Information about this can be obtained from your market research.

2.1 Purpose of the business

What are the objectives of your business and what are your values? As a therapist your "mission" (to use the jargon) may be to relieve people in your area from back pain or stress or whatever area you are specialising in.

2.2 Business founders and skill sets

Give a brief description of who you are, your skills, roles you are going to undertake and any past successes relevant to the business. It is important you identify achievements not just give chronological job descriptions. If other people are working for you, or with you, this is the place to describe their skill sets and their roles in the business. If there are obvious weaknesses in your management or business skills, you need to set out how you propose to deal with those weaknesses.

2.3 Competitive differential.

In essence how your business fits in with the market, how it is different and how it will be branded. If you have a logo or trademark, this is the time to use it, stating how relevant that is in the market.

Section 3: Products And Services

In this section you need to specify your service or product and how you plan to grow the business.

3.1 Product or service

You need to give a simple description of your service and/or products. If you have developed a new methodology for provision of service (maybe you merge cognitive behavioural techniques with hypnotherapy, for example, and you may want to brand that) state that and detail any trademarks or patent applied for.

3.2 Future growth

What other services will be developed or new products are being considered, and what are the barriers to entry to the market, if any? For future potential, how are you going to build your business?

An investor will be looking for growth in value of the business. As an individual you can only work so many hours a week and therefore the maximum you can earn is the available hours multiplied by your charge-out rate. If being busy and earning that amount is your criteria for success that is fine. However, if you wish to grow your business you need to think how you are going to "leverage" your time or money by tapping into others' resources. For example you may wish to set up a clinic and have other therapists who either rent a room or you employ; or you may wish to sell complementary products (aromatherapy oils, Chinese herbs, nutritional supplements, books, DVDs).

Section 4: Markets

The purpose of this section is to show how the business operates within the existing marketplace, the size of the market, its location, the possibilities of growth, customers and the estimated market share the business hopes to obtain. This is one of the most critical sections in the whole business plan and if a bank or investor is looking at your business they will want to ensure that you have done a lot of market research into both your products or services and the competition. [See **Module 2** *on market research.]*

4.1 Geographic spread

Where is the business located and how broad is its reach? For a clinic this would generally be a smaller catchment area than for someone who is mobile.

4.2 Market history

What has the market been like in the past? Is it still growing or has it levelled out?

4.3 Market size

What is the size of the market? This can be done in terms of potential customers, or analysed into sector in which the niche is positioned.

4.4 Possibilities of growth

Although there are different growth models, successful businesses tend to go through a number of stages:

a.   generate repeat sales;

b.   find new customers;

c.   develop competitive advantage based on the unique selling proposition in the target market

d.   develop long-term relationships and networks. It is at this point the staff are usually recruited and the owner needs to think more strategically about the business, where it is going, and whether you need further funding. From the research that I have done, therapists who are successful reach a stage where they can no longer take on more clients (or maybe feel they cannot take on more clients, due to the nature of the work). In order to grow the business a therapist must look at achieving different streams of income. This could be by providing different therapies to existing clients, earning money from writing articles or teaching, or taking on additional therapists, for example.

4.5 Customers

Who are your customers? How do they buy from you? What are their problems that you are trying to solve? Are they the decision-makers or do other people make decisions for them, for example parents?

4.6 Competitors

Who are your competitors? Where are they located? Taking two or three main competitors in particular, look at their strengths and weaknesses, their competitive advantages, their market share, and a prognosis of how they are likely to respond to your challenge.

4.7 Market share

What market share do you estimate your business will achieve? Obviously the more that you define your niche, the larger market share you can achieve.

Section 5: Marketing

The objective of this section is to show how you intend to market the services, describe why you have chosen that particular marketing method, how you know that you are going to be successful and the costs involved. You will need to state your pricing policy and how you test that in the marketplace.

5.1 Promotion

How do you intend to promote your services? What will it cost? You will need to have done some secondary research on the costs of various marketing areas such as advertising, discounts, getting flyers printed and delivered etc. You will need to show that you have explored different promotional methods such as:

- internet,
- direct mail,
- telephone selling,
- sales promotions,
- advertising,
- direct selling,
- using affiliates,
- other methods appropriate for your particular marketplace.

5.2 Test and measure

For every method of marketing and promotion that you do, you should test the response rate and how many new clients you get from that (called the "conversion rate" in the jargon).

5.3 Sales pitch and benefits of the product or service

What are the benefits of your products or services and how are you going to display that, and market that?

5.4 Sales expectations

How many clients do you expect to see and over what period? Is the income likely to be seasonal? (For example, as a sports massage therapist specialising in rugby players you may find you have a shortage of clients during the summer months, so you may also need to specialise in a summer sport such as massage for tennis players).

5.5 Market position

What is your position in the marketplace in relation to the competition? What that means is: are you going for high-end, high-quality, high price, or discount high volume, low price?

5.6 Prospective customers

In your early market research how much interest has been shown in your therapy and by which type of customers?

5.7 Pricing

How have you arrived at your pricing? (see **Module 7** on pricing and charging fees).

Section 6: Operations

The objective of this section is to cover the location and the equipment that you need to set up. For example if you could be working from a clinic you need to specify the clinic and why you have chosen that; or if you need to buy equipment you need to specify what you have chosen and why.

6.1 Location

Where will you be based? How much will it cost? Do you need a license? Have you read through the contract? Is it short-term or long-term? Why did you choose the location?

6.2 Supplies

Specify your sources of supply of key materials and equipment.

6.3 Information Technology

What is your information technology strategy? See **Module 11** on websites.

Section 7: Management

This is particularly key as investors are particularly interested in the skills, motivation and ability of the management team. They will need to know the experiences and skills and knowledge and whether there are any gaps within the team—and you need to show how those can be plugged.

7.1 Business Owners

Who are the business owners? Include their CVs (resumés) in an appendix.

7.2 Staff

What are the skills and knowledge base of all staff and where are the gaps? How are these gaps going to be filled?

Section 8: Finance

This section should be written after the rest of the sections because it is translating the rest of the plan in monetary terms. You will not be able to complete all the parts until you have done your market research, marketing plan and are clear where you are going to be located.

8.1 Forecasts

You will need to show your profit/loss account, the contribution and break-even analysis, cash flow analysis, sensitivity analysis and balance sheets for between three and five years. (See **Module 12**).

8.2 Assumptions

What are the assumptions that you have made in preparing the accounts?

8.3 Risks

What are the principal risks that could affect the figures?

8.4   Funds

What funds are required and when? What are the terms of the deal:

what interest rates are being charged?

is the loan fixed rate or floating?

what are the payment periods?

what guarantees are there?

what are the types of financing?

what (or who) is the source of finance?

what is the exit route for investors?

8.5   SWOT analysis

Produce a SWOT analysis—that is, strengths of the business, weaknesses, opportunities and threats (see my website: this is available as a separate download).

Section 9: Risks and Rewards

This section looks at the risks and how management intends to minimise these. It covers not just financial risks but also other risks, for example competition, or key worker critical illness. The rewards cover the position if the projected profit materialises, how will the business change?

9.1   Risks
9.2   Rewards

Section 10: Objectives and Milestones

The purpose of this section is to give a detailed timetable for the action plan in each area. In addition, you should cover your personal objectives about running a business, how you intend to achieve its objectives, what objectives you have for the business itself and how you intend to achieve them.

10.1 Milestone plan (See template)
10.2 Personal objectives

10.3 Business objectives

Appendices

Appendices can include any technical data, market research reports, marketing plan, CV of owner or owners, and detailed financial projections including cash flow forecasts.

Summary and Conclusions

It is worth while going through the process of doing the business plan yourself even if you do not have any investors as it should be clear to you by the time you've finished whether or not you have a viable business—if, of course, you have realistic forecasts!

Three Questions You Need to Ask Yourself

At the end of this process you should be to answer the following three questions:

1. What is your business about?
2. How do you help people?
3. Why should I buy from you?

If you are still not clear about each of these questions, you need to do some more research before starting a business; otherwise you are going to waste a lot of time money and energy on a business that becomes another failure statistic.

Module 6:
Location, Location, Location
Home, clinic or mobile?

One of the key decisions that you will need to make is where you wish to carry on your business. Do you intend to work from home? Rent a room in a clinic? Set up a clinic or spa? Or go mobile?

Home
The **advantages** of working from home include:
- no travelling
- you can suit your own hours
- you have flexibility
- you can make a relaxed environment, to put people at ease
- you can offset some of your utility bills etc against your tax bill
- you have full control over the decoration and feel of the place.

The **disadvantages** of being at home are:
- you need to have a dedicated use of the room and bathroom (although for business rates and potential capital gains tax problems it is preferable to have a dual use room—see separate sections)
- you need to consider extra insurance
- consider whether the room can be made accessible as required under the Disability Discrimination Act (see **Module 4**)
- you also need to consider issues such as cleanliness and tidiness, as well as noise and interruptions from the rest of the household

- you need to consider the health and safety issues and security of yourself and property
- it is also worthwhile checking under the terms of your mortgage that you are allowed to carry on the business in the home. Sometimes there are restrictions under the deeds of your house, so again it is worthwhile checking it out.

Clinic (i.e. renting space)

The **advantages** of using a clinic are:

- it projects a more professional image
- you may have a receptionist who can deal with payments and make appointments on your behalf, and who can be a bit of a buffer between you and the client
- there is little preparation or cleaning required
- the premises will already have any appropriate licences and insurances (apart from your professional indemnity insurance of course)
- there is an opportunity for cross-referring or supervision from other members of the clinic, and a sense of teamwork
- if the clinic has a good reputation that will reflect on you

The **disadvantages** of being in a clinic are that:

- it is usually more expensive than running the business from home
- you will have less control of the room layout and decoration
- you may have additional contractual obligations. For example you may need to be *in situ* from early in the morning until late at night, or have to pay for the full day, even if you only have one or two clients in that day
- if your business is going well and the clinic is only available one day a week you may struggle to grow your income
- if the clinic has a bad reputation that will reflect on you
- there may be possibilities of personality clashes.

Key things to look at in a contract to rent a room in a clinic

The key thing with the clinic is to be very clear what is covered and what is excluded in the contract that you sign. Issues you need to consider are:

1. What is the duration of the contract?
2. Are you agreeing to hire the room for a half or full day or on an hourly basis?
3. If you are hiring a room on an hourly basis how easy is it to obtain the room at the time you want? Will it be the same room each time?
4. If you are hiring the room for a half or full day are you permitted to sublet it to other therapists?
5. What is included in the cost of the rent:
   a) rental of the room, with or without equipment?
   b) the use of the receptionist?
   c) advertising and marketing?
   d) decoration?
   e) use and laundry of towels (even if you don't use them!)?
6. What are your obligations under the terms of the contract? Are you:
   a) expected to be there from eight in the morning till nine at night, even if you don't have any clients?
   b) expected to contribute to and be part of staff meetings and demonstration evenings?
   c) expected to adhere to clinic policies on charging, use of discounts, concessions etc?
   d) expected to staff the reception area for free for a period of time in the week?
7. How is the rent calculated: is it a set fee; different at peak times; based on a percentage of your income?

Factors to consider when deciding on a clinic

You need to check the terms of the contract in fine detail and be very clear what your costs and obligations are, the length of your lease, the notice period and what the restrictions are.

In deciding whether to set up your own clinic or join an established clinic you will need to consider the factors of where your business is to be located in comparison to your market. For example if your niche market is for lower-income, stressed mothers who do not have access to a car, then finding a clinic close to good public transport may be key. If you intend to have as your niche local people who drop in without an appointment it is all important that you are in a location which has what is termed a "good foot-fall", in other words in a busy street full of potential clients.

Also reflect on: how easy is it to park? Will clients have to pay for parking? How easy is it for you to gain access to carry your heavy equipment? It is worthwhile going and standing outside the proposed clinic at different times of day to see how busy it is and how many people are going in off the street. If you're not known to the owners, go in and get a sense of the place, what's the atmosphere like to work in? Does it seem professional or relaxed? Does that fit your style or not?

Mobile working

The **advantages** of mobile working are:
- flexibility
- you can work the hours to suit you
- low overheads
- some clients really value the home visit (for example in my accountancy I specialised in individuals who had mobility problems and one of my key selling points was that I would visit people in their own home). It is often good for the client because they can just relax after the therapy and don't have to drive.

The **disadvantages** of mobile working are:

* it can be quite time-consuming in terms of the travel, setup and the potential for chitchat
* as you will not be able to complete as many sessions each day that will need to be factored into the fees that you charge, for example, you may charge extra travel time
* you'll need to consider your personal safety and security
* it may be physically tiring, especially if you need to carry a heavy couch up three flights of stairs!
* you can also have a sense of isolation because of the lack of contact with colleagues
* you have less control over the environment.

Summary and Conclusion

Whichever method of working you choose, you can of course mix and match. For example if you are just setting up you may decide to hire a clinic initially on an hourly basis or perhaps even have half a day. As your business expands you may want to take on a full day in one or more clinics and to expand further you may decide that you will invite some of your more regular clients and give them the option to come to your home. To get around the disability access issues some therapists offer the option of having a mobile service if required.

Module 7:
Money, Money, Money
Setting your prices to make a profit

If you are in business, you need to make a profit. In order to increase your profit you have to:

a)   increase the number of sales that you make, or

b)   increase the price that you charge on each sale, or

c)   change the mix of the services (sell more of the profitable services or goods) that you provide, or

d)   decrease your costs.

In your market research that you have done, you will have obtained and set up a database of competitors and what they are charging. Just in case you haven't done it, now would be a good time...

You will need to note whether they offer additional services or longer sessions, their pricing policy and whether they offer concessions.

Let's assume that you are going to set up an acupuncture business in an already established clinic that does not have an acupuncturist already (although it can be for any therapy, of course). The clinic may not have a licence needed by the council so you will probably have to apply for that; you will also need to bear in mind additional costs that you may need to set up (a sink, proper waste disposal for sharps, etc.).

Calculating Fees

One way of calculating the fees that you will need to charge are to "reverse-engineer" the figures from what you want to make, to work out what you need to charge per session.

In the first instance you will need to calculate all of your costs for a year that you anticipate and then decide how much profit you would like to make in order to live on. Don't forget that you will need to pay taxes! This will also need to be a cost that you include. In the UK as a general rule of thumb you should set aside 30% of your income for income tax and National Insurance.

It might be easiest to show by way of an example.

Suppose that you estimate that all of your costs for the year will be £8,000, including depreciation (the wear-and-tear on your equipment) and taxes, and that you would like to earn £12,000. That means that you will need to earn £20,000 in the year to cover your costs (£8,000) and to give yourself the income (£12,000).

If you are going to be working for 48 weeks in the year, to give yourself four weeks' holiday:

£20,000 divided by 48 equals £417 per week

If you are going to be working five days a week you need to take your weekly total and divide that by five:

£417 per week divided by five equals £83 per day

If you do 4 sessions a day you need to divide £83 by four:

£83 per day divided by four equals £21.

(Obviously you can insert your own figures into the above calculations.)

This means that you will need to charge £21 as a minimum for each session, to do four sessions a day and work five days a week for 48 weeks in order to make £12,000 income and to cover your costs of £8,000.

Breakeven calculation

Assume that you charge £21 per session, but you find that you are not getting enough clients to do four sessions a day. You are concerned that you will not be able to cover all of your costs. So you can calculate how many sessions you will need to do in order to cover all of your costs.

Costs can be split into two: those that will stay the same however many sessions you do (fixed costs) and those costs that fluctuate with how many sessions you do (variable costs). Examples of fixed costs would be your subscription to your regulatory body, your rent (if you pay a fixed amount five days a week irrespective of how many clients you get). Variable costs might include couch roll, taxes (if you set aside 30%) and rent, if you are in the lucky position that you only pay for a room when you have a session.

To calculate the breakeven quantity (which is a posh way of saying how many sessions you need to do in order to cover your costs) you need to divide the fixed costs by the "contribution per unit"— that is, the sales price less the variable costs per unit.

In our example let us suppose that the variable costs (including taxes) are £7 per session and the fixed costs are £5,280.

The contribution (profit to you and me) per unit will therefore be £14 per session (£21 price less £7 variable cost).

The breakeven quantity will therefore be:

$$\frac{\text{Fixed costs}}{\text{Contribution per unit}}$$

...or, in this case:

$$\frac{5,280}{14} = 377.143$$

The breakeven quantity is 378. In other words, you need to do 378 sessions in the year to cover your fixed costs. Every session that you do over 378, you will make a profit of £14.

Thinking this through, this means that you should try and keep your fixed costs as low as possible.

Other Factors in Setting Fees

The trouble with the fee calculation is that it does not take into consideration that you might not be able to get four sessions a day, five days a week for that period of time, or that you might wish to charge a range of prices for different people, for example a lower rate for the over 60s and the unemployed, and a higher rate for those who are more wealthy.

To set the price you also need to consider the following:

a) How your service compares with competitive services, for example, if you are a massage therapist do your competitors also offer aromatherapy massage?

b) The life cycle of the service—is it new or mature? Obviously the therapist who is well established and well known and has a very good reputation has a much greater demand for their services and therefore can charge a higher price.

c) How price-sensitive are your customers? Statistics have shown that although customers say that they want lower prices particularly for something like therapy, people are often very loyal to their existing therapists. Generally customers will stay with a therapist unless they feel they are no longer getting value for money, feel they no longer need the service, or feel dissatisfied with the overall service. Unfortunately a number of clients just stop coming, and unless you follow up with them you will not know why they left. The more your customers feel they are getting an individual, differentiated (unique) service the more value they will place on that, and the more they are willing to pay for and be loyal to you as a therapist.

d) What is the price saying about your brand and the quality of your service? Clients often associate higher quality with a higher price, for example top health resorts can charge 60 or 70 per cent more per treatment than one delivered on a local high street.

e) How does your service fit within the local market? Is there more demand than supply (in which case you can demand a higher price)? Or are there already some well-established market leaders who can meet the demand in the local market? In these difficult competitive markets it is absolutely critical that you can differentiate your service from those provided by the market leaders. For example, can you be more flexible in terms of working hours? Do you specialise in a particular therapy which is not so well known in your particular market (examples might be Hawaiian massage or Thai massage)? You may be particularly good at relating to children or young people and you can use this to differentiate your service.

Controlling costs

Obviously, if you charge a higher price near the top end of the range you would be expected to provide a higher quality service or a more differentiated service. In order to be profitable you need to be very clear where all of your costs are being incurred, and what benefits you are deriving from each of your costs.

If you're scratching your head at this point and thinking how on earth can you get benefits from costs, one unorthodox way to look at costs is to look at each cost and decide what does that give you in terms of benefit and can you measure that?

Obviously there are some costs that you need to incur in order to do business, such as insurances and regulatory costs, and the benefit of that is that they give you the opportunity to actually set up and maintain your business; other costs will be incurred that may be seen to be more discretionary. An example of discretionary costs may be the choice to have fresh flowers in the room, or music, or particular decoration in order to give the ambience that you require.

When setting up it is very easy to overspend on these more discretionary items. Therefore, ask yourself before you buy something, how many hours work will I need to do in order to obtain this item? Using our example from above your contribution (profit) per unit is £14, thus an item costing £28 will need 2 hours' work to cover the cost. Is the benefit from having that item worth two hours' work?

An area where it is easy to lose control of costs is in marketing and advertising. In **Module 10**, the marketing module, we will be looking at measuring your advertising and marketing spend and there you will need to consider how many clients you need to achieve in order to cover the costs of advertising, and how many new clients you are achieving for each different promotion.

What Do your Competitors Charge?

Many new therapists start by undercutting the competition and charging lower fees. This may be partly due to fear (or a belief that the main factor in buying is price, when that is not necessarily the case; people like to feel they are getting value for money). Once you have set your prices it is very difficult to then put them up again when you have your clients, so I advise people to set an appropriate price, perhaps with a range for the unemployed or the elderly as long as you have corresponding number of people who are paying the full rate. Obviously the more market research you have done beforehand, the more you know about your target market, the more likely you are to be able to understand what they are looking for in the service and be able to supply that.

As of late summer 2009, in my local vicinity, Bristol in the UK, the prices that I have seen quoted from the research that I have done are:

Osteopathy, 30 minutes	*average £35*
Sports injury, one hour	*range £35–£45*
Physiotherapy, 30 minutes	*average £35*
Acupuncture, 30 minutes	*range £35–£42*
Psychotherapy and counselling, 50 minutes	*range £30–£42*
Chiropractor, 30 minutes	*average £35*
Hypnotherapy, 45 minutes	*average £35*
Dietetics, 30 minutes	*average £35*
Chinese herbal remedies, 30 minutes	*average £42*
Homoeopathy, 30 minutes	*range £37–£40*
Kinesiology, 30 minutes	*average £35*
NLP and coaching, 45 minutes	*range £35–£60*
Thai massage, one hour	*average £42*
Shiatsu, one hour	*average £40*
Swedish/holistic massage, one hour	*range £35–£42*
Deep tissue massage, one hour	*average £40*
Reflexology, one hour	*range £30–£38*
Reiki, one hour	*range £30–£38*
Aromatherapy, one hour	*average £35*
Indian head massage, 30 minutes	*range £22–£30*
Ear candling, 30 minutes	*range £22–£24*
Ayur yogic massage, one and a half hours	*average £60*

Obviously, where you are there will be differences, but that gives you a view of the spread of some of the key therapies that are available on the market. It is interesting to note that those that deal with immediate acute pain, for example osteopathy and sports injury, command the highest prices. Most of the therapies will charge extra for the initial consultation, which typically lasts half an hour.

When doing research on the above I also checked the cancellation or missed appointment policy. Almost without exception most specified in their brochures or on their websites that they needed 24 hours' notice, otherwise the full fee would be payable.

What do I do if my client cancels within 24 hours, or misses an appointment?

Seven top tips from various practicing therapists are:

1. Ask for a non-refundable deposit when they book the appointment so at least you get partial payment.

2. Try a "three strikes and you're out" policy, that is if they miss three appointments they will no longer be able to book an appointment until they have paid up for those missed appointments.

3. If you have a receptionist, ask him or her to contact the individual the day before to check whether they are coming and confirm the appointment.

4. Get people to sign a piece of paper when they first arrive at their first appointment that states that they will accept that they will be liable if they do not show up for an appointment.

5. Take the client's credit card number and state that they will be charged in full if they do not turn up for an appointment. You can take credit cards through PayPal for a small(ish) percentage. Usually taking the credit card number in itself is sufficient deterrent to not miss the appointment.

6. Say to people they can give their appointment to a friend or colleague (or sell it on eBay?!). As long as someone comes along and pays for the session... and who knows, you may get a new client that way!

7. Keep a list of people who regularly miss appointments and give them lower priority times etc. You need to be a little careful with this as people can pick up energies, particularly if they are negative!

Summary and Conclusions

You will need to decide your pricing policy bearing in mind how differentiated your service is, how much your competitors charge and how much money you wish to make.

Module 8:
Cash is King
Cash Flow Forecasting

• • • ●

As the saying goes, "cash is king." What that means is that some businesses go out of business not because they are not profitable, but because they do not have the cash to pay their suppliers, or their tax bill, and they're still waiting to be paid by their customers.

As of late summer 2009, the current economic climate is not ideal for obtaining bank overdrafts and credit (see **Module 9** on funding). Banks are still very jittery on commercial lending and therefore will be very quick not just to charge for an unauthorised overdraft, but may be much quicker on closing a businesses bank account. Her Majesty's Revenue and Customs are also responsible for a large number of business closures in a year, by which I mean the owners have not set aside sufficient cash to pay either their tax bill or their VAT bill when it is due.

It is really important, then, that you have an idea of what is coming into your bank account and what is going out of your bank account. For this purpose you need to draw up a cash flow forecast. A cash flow forecast shows you month-by-month what you expect to go into and out of the business each month. The difference between the cash coming in over the cash going out is called the net inflow or outflow. The net inflow will be added to the bank balance at the start of the month to show the bank balance at the end of the month. That is the figure that will be carried forward to the next month.

Cash or Credit?

I strongly recommend that you as a therapist do not offer any credit terms (that they can pay you at a later time) to any of your customers. This may sound harsh but you do need to be paid up front for the work that you have done. Some therapists will accept credit cards, although credit card companies charge a fee, usually between 2% and 4% of the total amount, for the use of a credit card service. You'll need to consider whether the fee charged is worthwhile for the extra convenience of your clients if you wish to offer that service.

In my experience in the first year of trading a rule of thumb is that income is half of what is expected and expenditure is twice what is expected. This may sound cynical but at least it gives you an idea of the potential problem if you do not have enough cash to pay your immediate **creditors** (the people you owe money to). I strongly suggest that you prepare your cash flow forecast based on the fact that it may take you twice as long to cover your costs as you originally anticipate.

What is included in a cash flow forecast?

A cash flow forecast can easily be done in something like an Excel spreadsheet (or on a piece of paper if you hate computers) and shows the expected payments into the bank account and payments out of your bank account on a month-by-month basis.

Ideally a business plan will include a monthly cash flow forecast for the first year if not two years. At the end of each month you should check the estimated figures with the actual receipts and costs that you incurred in the month. It is worth reviewing your cash flow forecast monthly and amending it as necessary.

Receipts

You need to show:
- your cash from sales,
- any interest earned in the bank account,

- any payment of capital into the bank account (the amount you invest in the business in the first place)
- sale of assets and
- any other receipts and payments you have made in to your bank account for a particular month.

Add up all your income and receipts to give a total receipts figure.

Payments

You need to include:

- payments to suppliers, including rents and rates,
- cash purchases
- any drawings (the amount you pay yourself as a form of salary)
- any tax payments
- insurances
- advertising and marketing
- heating and lighting
- stationery
- professional fees
- telephone and internet
- general expenses
- bank interest
- any loan repayments and
- other payments for a particular month.

Add all of your payments from your bank account to give a total payments figure.

Net inflow or outflow

Take the total receipts figure calculated above, minus the total payments figure per month, to arrive at the net inflow or outflow into the bank account.

Opening bank balance

This figure is the amount you actually had in your business bank account at the start of the month. If you owe money to the bank than this figure should be shown as a minus figure or in brackets. At the start of trading the opening bank balance is likely to be nil.

The opening bank balance for one month will be the closing bank balance from the previous month.

Continue this for each month for a minimum of 12 months. If you are unsure when cash payments are going to be made out, it is safer to put payments earlier and show receipts later.

Some cash flow forecasts do not show a figure for actuals, that is, what happened in reality. I recommend that you include a column for actuals each month, as it gives you something to compare and measure against and you can see how you are doing against your forecast. This is important, for example, if you find you have not made the sales that you anticipated, at least you can take some action to either increase sales and reduce costs or reduce your drawings (your salary) or possibly to obtain extra funding before you get into trouble with the banks for going overdrawn without permission.

In the actual figures column you transfer the figures from your cash book to your cash flow forecast.

You can also show an additional column for each month, which compares the forecast figures with the actual figures. This column is usually referred to as the variance. You do not have to do this formally but it can be useful. For example if you assume that your sales were going to be £400 in one month and the actual sales were £210 you have got a shortfall already of £190 (which would be shown in the variance column). You need to decide how you are going to make up that shortfall... will you attempt to make more sales next month, or reduce your costs?

Bank Reconciliations

At the end of the month when you receive your bank statement you should be able to check off all of the items against your bank statement and at the end they should be reconciled . You can prepare a bank reconciliation each month that analyses the difference between your cashbook figures and the figures per the bank statement. The difference is usually receipts you have made into the bank, or cheques you have written that have not been "presented" to the bank and consequently that have not been shown on the bank statement. Don't forget to include bank charges and bank interest in your actual figures!

Profit and Loss

Profit is not the same as cash. A profit (or loss) is produced by taking the difference between sales and costs in a particular period, for example a year. It is possible to make a profit and have no cash, for example, where you have had to pay cash up front for rent in advance, stationery supplies, wages and salaries.

Balance Sheet

A balance sheet shows the assets and liabilities of the business at a point in time. Assets include your long-term assets, such as a massage table. Long-term assets are called "**fixed assets**". Those that are easily converted into cash, such as stock of product, cash balances, debtor balances (where your clients owe you money) are called "**current assets**". Fixed assets and current assets added together give you your "total assets". **Liabilities** include items those items where you owe an amount to suppliers or the tax authorities, but you have not yet paid over the figures.

The total net assets (total assets less total liabilities) give you an indication of the worth of the business.

I do not intend to say much more about the balance sheet at this stage, as most therapists do not need to produce one, as they do not do business through a company.

Summary and Conclusions

When you are preparing your business plan you will need to do a cash flow forecast. For control and management purposes at the end of each month you should insert the cash that you actually received and paid out and compare that with the figures per the bank statement.

From a business point of view you need to be very strong in controlling your costs and ensure that you are deriving a benefit for incurring that cost.

Module 9:
Please Sir, can I have some more?
Obtaining Finance

∙
∙
∙
●

So you have done your cash flow forecast and you realise that you need to get funds from somebody to tide you over till you start making money, or to buy equipment. There are two sorts of finance: short-term finance and long-term finance.

Short-term Finance

If you are a self-employed therapist renting a fully-equipped room in a clinic, you probably do not have high initial financial requirements. Remember, though, that you need to find not just your (long-term) capital expenditure, that is on your equipment, but also your "working capital". Working capital is the funding you need to operate on a daily basis. You can think of it as the amount to cover the gap between when you have to pay your suppliers, for the room, marketing and when you have sufficient cash from your customers to cover all your costs. Beware, there will almost certainly be a longer period of time than you expect to build up the level of customers and it is really worthwhile making contingency plans to cover additional delay.

The initial funding is probably the most critical and most difficult to obtain as you do not have any credit-worthiness that a bank or other lender will be able to take comfort from; it is probably the most difficult to predict and unfortunately it is also the most difficult to hold onto!

Treat each pound spent as though it is golden. What you don't want to do is drop into unauthorised overdrafts, were you get charged not just interest rates but also a penalty.

Overdrafts

Even with authorised overdrafts, as of late summer 2009 the main banks typically charge about 19% interest, which means if you have a £1000 overdraft, overdrawn 15 days each month, the interest is about £90-£100 a year.

There are some deals such as Alliance+Leicester's deals, which give you a 0 percent overdraft, but you do have to pay 50p a day service charge if you do use the overdraft after a time period. For more details go to what must be the best overall website in the UK for money advice. It is unbiased and it's free and there is a great forum where you can ask questions. The website is http://www.moneysavingexpert.com (I strongly recommend that you have a look at that for your personal finances too!)

Remember that overdrafts are also treated as debt. If you regularly go into overdraft it will affect the credit rating of you or your business. In the short term (a month or two at most) overdrafts can be more expensive than using credit cards so if you are close to the limit it may be worthwhile thinking of using your credit card and paying that off in the following month.

Long-term Finance

Family or Friends loan (or Self Financed)

This is the way most people start up. There are a number of advantages and disadvantages that are shown below.

Bank Loan

If you can obtain a bank loan you will almost certainly have to show the bank your business plan (and they will check on a regular basis that you are managing your business to the business plan) and may have to give a form of personal guarantee for the loan (often secured on your home).

With a bank loan you will be supplied with a fixed cash amount and will have to pay back a fixed amount each month that will be interest and part of the capital repayment. As with all loans for business purposes you can offset the interest on your loan against your tax bill. You will need to show that the loan was used for business purposes.

If you can't get any bank accounts because of poor credit rating it is worthwhile exploring the Co-operative Bank, who seem to be more accommodating than most to set up a basic bank account (you can pay money in and out and have a card to withdraw cash but you do not get a credit card).

Grants

If you can get a grant they are absolutely the best way to go because you don't have to pay them back! It is worth checking out the following:

- **New Deal:** Government scheme for those currently on the unemployed register
- **Prince's Trust:** although this is primarily for young entrepreneurs (up to 30) there is a also a scheme for mature people (over 50) setting up their own business, called Prime. See http://www.princeofwales.gov.uk/personalprofiles/theprinceofwales/atwork/theprincescharities/opportunityandenterprise/
- **Regional Development Agency**
- **Local Authorities**
- **Chambers Of Commerce**
- **Local Enterprise Board** (for example BRAVE in Bristol)
- **Business Link** occasionally used to give out a small grant towards setting up a website. You'd need to check whether this is available

locally, although I do know that some people have not been able to get hold of it more recently. Business Link does have a search facility for grants so you can check if there are any that you would be eligible for. As far as I'm aware there are no grants that are specifically set out for therapists or to encourage therapists. If you know differently, please let me know!

Advantages and Disadvantages of Different Finance

Loans from friends or family
Advantages:
- can be more flexible
- any interest payments made to the family member stay within the family
- they are unlikely to require any formal security (or force you to sell your house if you don't pay up).

Disadvantages:
- the family member may feel they can interfere in the business
- if the business fails it can make family relationships very difficult
- the family member may need the funds for other uses and demand immediate payment. This happened to one of my clients despite having a written agreement: her father-in-law required early repayment as he needed to finance his own daughter's wedding! The struggle to find funds and the additional costs almost resulted in the business collapsing.

Bank Loans
Advantages:
- the rate of interest is usually lower than for an overdraft
- usually the term of the loan (that is how long it is outstanding for) is known in advance

- it can be easier to obtain a bank loan particularly if you have got a good credit rating and already have a bank account with that particular bank
- usually the repayment schedule split between capital (the repayment of the loan) and the interest are known in advance.

Disadvantages:
- you will need to pay the interest and capital repayments even if you do not have the funds to pay them from the business. You will therefore need to have good cash flow forecasts to ensure you can cover all the repayments and/or have access to other funds to ensure that you do not fall foul of the repayments
- it is more difficult to get hold of bank loans at the moment, particularly for new businesses, as they are considered to be high risk
- even if you can obtain a bank loan it may need to be secured against your personal assets—usually your home. Potentially you could lose your home if you do not pay your loan repayments.

Bank Overdrafts
Advantages:
- they are useful in the short term
- you only pay interest and "service fee" when you actually go into overdraft, therefore overdrafts tend to be cheaper than loans if you only go into overdraft very occasionally,
- they are flexible, you choose when you use them

Disadvantages:
- they are repayable on demand,
- they will often be secured against business assets,
- they often attract a very high interest rate (see above), and if you exceed the overdraft limit you will enter the realm of penalties, which can be very severe.

Lease/HP

This is where you make payments over the life of a major asset and in the final payment the ownership transfers to you (HP) or never transfers to you (with a lease).

Advantages:

- security is only on the assets purchased, not on the whole business

Disadvantages:

- tends to be very expensive,
- you will need good cash flow forecasts to ensure you can cover all the repayments or have access to other funds to ensure that you do not fall foul of repayments.

Other Finance Forms

There are other forms of financing which are not usually available to therapists, but I have included them as you may hear reference to them.

a) **Factoring.** Sales invoices are bought by factoring companies for a fee, giving you immediate cash for your debtors. These are not really relevant to therapists as you should get cash up front from your clients, not be running an invoice-based business!

If you have a company there are other forms of finance available:

b) **issuing shares** in the company and giving away some of the value of the business to external shareholders,

c) going to "**business angels**" who are people who don't just invest in companies but also tend to mentor the owners of the companies. *Dragon's Den* is an example of people who act as business angels. The name of course does not imply that their behaviour is going to be angelic!

Current Position for Obtaining Finance

As of late summer 2009, bank lending to small firms has decreased quite dramatically as banks are reassessing their risks and there is less money in the economy to go around.

That does not mean to say that you cannot obtain the funds; you may need to work harder in order to get them. The deals that you might have been able to negotiate in the past (lower interest rates or more favourable repayment terms) are not as attractive as they have been.

Taking a Business Plan to Finance Providers

If you do go to a bank or other finance provider with a business plan, these things are vital:

a)   make a well-presented business plan that has been well thought out

b)   look presentable and wear appropriate professional attire

c)   practice the presentation of your plan. You will need to think about the questions that you are likely to be asked, and how you will answer them. I recommend that you watch *Dragon's Den* on the BBC (or on YouTube). Think about what makes people credible and presentable, what questions were asked and what made people stumble. Practice with your friends or family beforehand, or if you are approaching more than one source of finance, look to the least hopeful chance first and use that as an excuse to hone your technique!

d)   make sure you know the facts and figures off by heart

e)   make sure you answer the questions that you have been asked

f)   if you are asked to provide further information, be very clear what it is that you need to present, research it well and provide it very quickly, within one or two days preferably

g)   remember to be enthusiastic about your business and what it is that is special about your particular business and you (your Unique Selling Proposition).

What are the Investors or Bank looking for?

The answer is *CAMPARI*!

Not that you need to bribe them with alcohol; it's an acronym:

CHARACTER
What is your business track record? What is your personal credit history? (Be aware a lot of investors will actually check your credit rating). Bankers will be trying to judge your honesty and integrity, whether you are true to your word. What are your values? They will also be looking to see if you have been realistic in your assumptions in your business plan.

ABILITY
Do you have the skills and knowledge and determination to make the business plan work as set down? This will cover your ability to manage your time and resources and quality and also your financial and business acumen.

MANAGEMENT
Do you have the necessary qualities in management? They will look at your education, experience, training and any relevant business experience that you have. If you do not have it yourself, have you shown how you will get it?

PURPOSE
Have you made it clear what you want the loan for? Is it in the best interests of the business? A friend of mine once applied to a bank for a loan to buy a light aircraft as he said that he could fly over potential properties to buy and develop. The bank was not impressed and said he could just as easily drive over and it was not in the best interests of the business to be spending the resources in this manner!

AMOUNT
Have you asked for the correct amount in your business plan presentation? Have you included all of the appropriate costs that you would expect? (For example, you might need to pay for loan arrangement fees etc) Have you put money in yourself? (Banks like to see that you have also invested as it shows that you will be more careful so that you do not lose your own funds). Have you put a contingency into the forecasts?

REPAYMENT
Will your business make enough money to repay all of the interest and capital in the correct time? Is the repayment term realistic?

INSURANCE
Is security necessary? Will your personal assets be required as security for the business loan?

Banks will also tend to look at basic financial data:

Breakeven Point. This is the quantity of sales or service at which the fixed costs are covered by the sales that are made. (See **"Breakeven calculation"on page 77**)

Interest Cover. This is (estimated) trading profit divided by interest for a period. If it is less than one, it is very risky. The higher the trading profit the higher the possibility of being able to pay the interest and the more comfortable the bank will be in lending you funds.

If you provide a balance sheet there is other financial data that bankers will look at. I have not included that here.

Ongoing monitoring by the banks

Even when you think you have got the funds, you can't just take the money and run! The banks will require regular contact and they will

- continue to look at your bank accounts
- expect you to produce accounts may be each quarter
- look at budgets for the following year, and
- look for any discrepancies between the forecasts and actuals.

The things that will make the bankers become very uncomfortable—
and therefore ask for either increased security, or higher interest payments, or even require early repayment of the loan—are as follows:

a)   frequently going over the overdraft limit. Have you been control-
      ling your cash flow properly?
b)   not providing financial information to the bank or being able to
      explain the figures
c)   forecasts being wildly out from the actual figures. Do you under-
      stand your business, do you understand the market?
d)   you are making yourself unavailable to talk to the bank manager.
      There is nothing like avoiding the phone calls to get a bank man-
      ager paranoid!
e)   poor profitability on an ongoing basis, declining sales and declin-
      ing margins.
f)   being over reliant on too few customers or suppliers. For exam-
      ple do you earn all of your income or the majority of your income
      from one business client? If they decide they no longer want to
      use your services there would be a huge impact on your business.

As a self-employed therapist you are unlikely to be eligible to have a
business angel investment as business angels are interested in taking
a part-share of the business in a company (that is, they invest with the
idea of taking some percentage share of the business when it grows).

Even though you may not be in the business of pure growth, yet you
may still want to have some support. Statistics have shown that businesses that have mentoring and coaching have a 20% greater chance of
surviving and thriving beyond three years, so you may want to consider
being mentored. In the first instance local enterprise trusts and Business Link can provide some services, or you can request the more per-

sonal one-to-one service of a business coach (such as I) offer. For more details please check my website, or send me an email:

e   gefwarren@gmail.com
w   http://www.setupatherapybusiness.com/

Summary and Conclusions

With regards to finance, the general rule is that you should have short-term loans or overdrafts to finance short-term assets (working capital); and long-term finance to purchase long-term assets such as equipment or property. What you don't want to do is mix.

It is more difficult to obtain finance at the moment, but if you have a credible business plan it is still possible to get the backing that you need.

Module 10:
Becoming a Client Magnet
Marketing

:
●

What is Marketing?

The Chartered Institute of Marketing defines marketing as the management process that is responsible for "identifying, anticipating and satisfying customer requirements profitably".

It is interesting that this doesn't say anything at all about selling, or that you have to meet everybody's needs, and it also adds that crucial word "profitably". If you are really serious about being in your business as a business you do need to make a profit. That doesn't mean to say you rip off your clients, far from it. In a service industry, such as therapy, it is about building long-term lasting client relationships. Your marketing strategy should reflect the need to build long-term relationships.

Research has shown that successful businesses attribute 50 per cent of their ongoing success to marketing. This is more than their knowledge and skill base, which accounts for 20 per cent or their personality at 30 per cent!

How do you do Effective Marketing?

Plan it

Marketing needs to be planned, needs to be consistent across different forms of marketing, and be applied consistently in the longer term.

Apply Longer Term
You can't just try something once, expect it to work and give up.

Be Consistent
As a therapist if you are going for a high-end, exclusive service, you don't want to be sending out direct mail shots on cheap, flimsy, translucent paper as this gives a completely different feel to the brand and image and that means customers will think that they can't trust you to deliver luxury that you are providing.

Don't be drawn in to pay for advertising you have not planned
If you ask most people what they consider to be marketing most people say advertising. However, advertising tends to be very expensive and isn't particularly targeted. When you first start off and you are short of clients, it is very easy, when you are phoned up by the local newspaper or magazine offering advertising, to say yes without thinking whether that is the best marketing strategy to go for.

Test All Your Marketing
It is really important that you don't just do one standard form of marketing. To be effective it should form part of an overall strategy. As with all marketing it is critical to measure and test the results and change the methods of marketing if they are not working.

Other forms of marketing are:
- direct mail
- internet marketing (which we will cover in **Module 11**)
- email marketing
- pay-per-click advertising
- newspaper and magazine advertising
- telephone marketing
- direct sales
- strategic alliances
- up-selling to existing customers or clients
- referral systems

- Public Relations (PR) type of marketing. PR includes network-ing, being associated with community activities and relationship marketing. Relationship marketing is key to services and it must be sincere and built on trust
- promotions in terms of leaflets and brochures
- point-of-sale displays
- mail shots
- newsletters: you can self-publish newsletters that give informa-tion and as long as they give value clients look forward to receiv-ing them
- press releases: the key to a press release is to take a different newsworthy angle to "sell" the story that makes it different
- TV and radio: tend to be very expensive. You can be talking about £1000 a week for a local radio advert and you need to get at least three weeks' worth to get any results
- word-of-mouth: for therapists (and other services) word-of-mouth recommendation and referrals are the best forms of mar-keting. Unfortunately, these take time to build up, which may be a deterrent when you first start. Therefore it's key that you ask for testimonials from your case studies when you were qualifying.

What are the best sort of testimonials?

Sometimes people are happy for you to write testimonials for them and for them to sign it based on what they've said. The kind of testimonial that works best are those that address people's fears: for example, where people say they were unsure about the therapy and that you reassured them, that they've had a really brilliant time or they felt very relaxed afterwards, or the concerns they had initially have now gone away.

Tips for testing and measuring promotional costs

1. Work out the cost per promotion. Promotion and marketing can be extremely costly and you need to know which is most effective, dropping the least effective and focusing on the more effective.

2. When you place an advert ask people to quote a particular code that relates to that magazine or paper. You also need to compare the response rate against the cost of that particular promotion.

3. If placing an advert never pay the "card rate" but negotiate a discount.

4. The best place for an advert in printed media is on the edge of the right page.

5. People learn by repetition: put two adverts in the same edition of a paper or journal as they will be remembered more than a single insertion. Similarly if you are to place an advert it is better to have a series in the same magazine.

6. Adverts are expensive; editorial is free—and the irony is that people believe the editorial much more than an advert where they feel they are being sold to. "Advertorials" are a half way house where you write a short piece of editorial and place an accompanying advert. Whenever you write a piece of editorial don't forget to include your website and contact details.

7. Write press releases when you have a story to tell, or write a series about your therapy and how that can help the readers of the magazine (examples have been aromatherapy for horse riders; reflexology for stress relief in a general practitioner's magazine).

Remember that sometimes people take a flyer or postcard or business card but will contact you some months (or even years!) later, therefore it is always worthwhile when people enquire asking them where they heard about you.

Six tips to increase the effectiveness of advertising in printed form (magazines, newspapers, directories)

1. **Barter:** In terms of advertising it is always worth negotiating the rates. To be effective, advertising should be for a series of inserts (people like familiarity), so use that fact to negotiate a better discount.

2. **Wait For It, Wait For It:** If you can wait very close to deadline date you can usually get better deals.

3.   **Choose Your Position:** Research shows that the best place for adverts is top right on the right-hand side of the page; if you do not have this place sometimes it is better to not advertise at all than have a more difficult (less effective)position.

4.   **Don't Be a Sheep:** Just because your competitors advertise in a particular magazine, or market themselves in a particular way, does not mean to say that you have to follow suit. In fact sometimes it is better to have a different strategy. In **Module 11** I'll talk in more detail about websites and using the Internet for marketing purposes—an area grossly under-represented by therapists.

5.   **Share the Costs:** If you are going to pay to advertise in any of the telephone directories the best one in terms of reach is Yellow Pages. However Yellow Pages is expensive. One way round this is to get together with people who have similar qualifications but may be practising in different locations within the Yellow Pages region so between you, you can afford a much bigger adverts which will draw the attention of the potential consumers. You may be able to use your regulatory body's logo (with permission of course!)

6.   **Dare to be Different:** Remember that you will be advertising where your competitors will be advertising, so ensure that you differentiate your service from theirs in your advert. For example, if you are more flexible on opening times, state that as a feature, so that potential customers can see a benefit to them... and if they are ringing round they will ask your competitors about opening times and decide that your times are more convenient.

One final thing: NEVER criticise your competitors—it will reflect badly on you and it is unprofessional. Let the customers decide for themselves.

Relationship Marketing

A critical marketing skill for therapists is long-term client relationship management. This means really getting to know your client very well: their needs, their concerns, their motivations and their life-style. See **Exercise 1—Client Analysis** later on in this module. It is crucial that the client feels important, that you listen to their views and opinions, that you understand their problems.

Alternative ("Guerrilla") Marketing

Other areas of marketing that can be really useful are:

Your Institute

You can become involved with your association or institute and become an active member and get yourself onto various subcommittees etc. For the time that it takes, you receive professional recognition from your peers, makes you stand out from others in the area, it gives you the semblance of being an expert, it is useful for networking, and of course you can make a real contribution towards building and developing a professional organisation!

Hobbies

If you have a particular hobby it can be useful to use your network of people as potential clients and to expand your business. People like people who are similar to them and obviously sharing interests is one way of building rapport. One of my students was a keen horse-rider and she wrote an article in the local horse magazine for which she got paid *and* also she gained extra kudos *and* gained some referrals from the article. If you do write an article, and I recommend that you do, remember to put your contact details at the end, including website.

Write Books or Articles

Research has shown that people will accept the word of "experts" and will seek the services of one they deem an authority in a particular discipline. I strongly recommend that you write articles or blogs and even a book to help increase your standing as an "expert" to gain credibility. You can also either give away or sell a copy to interested clients, building the relationship or making and additional income.

Testimonials

Recommendations and testimonials are by far the best publicity and promotion. Ask every satisfied client to recommend three acquaintances who may be interested in your services (if you ask for three, you may get one). It is important that you do the follow-up, not your client, so you need to approach a new prospect using the client's name, with their permission of course, as an introduction.

For testimonials ask your clients to put their comments in writing and to sign it. If they say they do not have the time, then write your own testimonial and ask them if they are happy with it. The most effective testimonials that those where people express concern at first about something (maybe a scepticism about the therapy) and then state that concern was allayed by their experience in the therapy as performed by you.

Maximise Different Income Streams

I strongly recommend that you consider as many different income streams as possible and also look to form strategic alliances with other people and other practices to your mutual advantage.

Links to Other Websites

If you have a website and you see someone else in a different area has a very good website with lots of information, why not link to that website and ask them to link to yours, as you will gain from having some information which is of real value to your potential customer, but because it is in your local area they will come back to you to ask for the appointment.

Focus on Customers' Problems with a Multi-Discipline Approach

Sometimes customers have common problems and very different practices can contribute to a solution. It can be to your advantage to link up with these other practices if necessary cross-refer or even offer joint sessions where people can try different therapies, for example, hypnotherapy and counselling for an addiction problem.

Sell Other Services or Products to Your Existing Clients

In terms of looking for new income streams, think about your current clients, what their problems are and what could potentially help them. For example, a lot of women struggle with eating and healthy lifestyle, perhaps you could get some further qualifications in nutrition, or sell books on nutrition as well as your own therapy.

Some "Dos And Don'ts" of Selling

Do not under any circumstances try the hard sell! If it doesn't work for second-hand car dealers it certainly won't work for a professional therapy practice. If you are desperate for a sale, potential clients will be able to smell it a mile off. It is crucial that you attract people to you who are desperate for your services.

Do not bad-mouth your competition or treat others with disrespect. You should always treat your practice and qualifications with the greatest professionalism and respect, for what you show, your clients will pick up also.

Do develop personal relationships with your clients, make them feel important and listened to.

Do make sure you are professional in approach at all times. If the initial contact is on the phone do not have noisy children, or the radio, or barking dogs in the background. If it is at your premises always ensure they are keen kept clean and tidy, the toilets are always spotless and modern, and you don't have strong disinfectants. If you have flowers, make sure they are kept fresh.

Do focus on the whole person, not just the specific problem. Research has shown that patients rarely talk to GPs about the real problem until about seven minutes into the conversation. It is probably very similar in the case of a therapist, if not more so, as some people are very wary about trusting complementary therapies.

Do build and maintain a favourable image and reputation to engender the personal loyalty. Potential clients tend to choose a specific person not a particular firm. They may trust a particular clinic, but the majority will want to see the same person again.

How to convert an enquiry by telephone or face-to-face

1. **Listen** to the enquirer. What are their concerns?
2. **Ask** open questions (why, where, when, what, how, whom) to help establish their problems and needs. It also helps to make them feel important.
3. **Establish their needs and wants.** A person will not always take up something that they need but largely they will take up something that they want. It is important you know the difference. An example is I need to buy myself a new pair of slippers, but I don't particularly want to change them as they are comfortable and I can wear them outside to take the bin out! On a less flippant note clients may need to diet, or give up drinking or smoking for health reasons but they may not want to. Unless someone really wants to change they will not change. The client may subsequently need to be coached in the alternatives open to them.
4. **Explain the benefits** that you provide to meet those wants or needs. If you cannot meet those wants, perversely, it can be to your advantage to refer them on to somebody who can, perhaps in an alternative therapy. In my experience when I have done this people have really appreciated my honesty and that I wasn't trying to rip them off and was genuinely interested in securing the best solution for their problem. In one instance we actually had two people referred back to us by a friend we had suggested to go elsewhere, so we got two clients for the loss of one!
5. **Close the deal.** It is worth trying the 'alternative close': "is it convenient this week or next?" The alternative close is usually by

way of a closed question and gives you information. If the potential customer objects then you can probe that objection, make it specific and try closing again. For example if they say it is too expensive, you may be able to say you offer reduced rates for the unemployed or the elderly, or may be able to suggest a shorter period of time, perhaps a half-hour session rather than a full hour session maybe?

6. Send or give literature and **follow up** with a telephone call or email to try and convert that to a sale later. Be very careful you do not appear desperate; it is absolutely critical that you seem concerned about their issues, not about your business!

To be successful you will need to be able to answer yes to the following:

1. Is your service created with the customer in mind?
2. Are you in business to make a profit?
3. Do you always deliver on your promises?
4. Do you know how you help your customers?
5. Do you always ask for testimonials or referrals?

What makes you better than or different from your competitors?

Is it:

1. Excellence of service?
2. Quality of product or experience?
3. Reputation and qualifications?
4. Image?
5. Your personality?
    (People buy from people that they like and feel rapport with.)
6. Price?
    (See **Module 7** on setting your price. Be very wary of offering discounts as research has shown that only 20% of people buy on the basis of price, whatever they say. At launch you may offer a lower price to induce people to come and try the service.)

Marketing Strategy

The main purpose of marketing is:

1. to build awareness
2. to differentiate yourself from your competitors
3. to build and maintain your overall image and reputation
4. to persuade customers to buy or use the service

In setting up your marketing strategy you need to be very clear of the purpose that you are targeting by that strategy. You also need to test your strategy. If you are setting up locally, and one of your USP points is that you are local and convenient, you might consider doing a mail drop around the local streets. Direct mail generally has only 1% to 2% "conversion rate" i.e. people who follow up the direct mail. If it is a service that people think they may need later stage, for example a chiropractor or an osteopath, they may keep your business card or brochure for use at a later date. It is really important that when people come to you, you ask them how they heard about you. If you do place adverts ask people to quote a particular reference number, which refers to the magazine or newspaper in which you advertised.

You need to have a very clear view of who your target market is. The more specific you are with your targets the more they will feel that you are talking to them specifically. It may be that one niche is not big enough, so you may need to target more than one niche. For example when I did accountancy I advertised locally, and I also specialised in therapists and therefore advertised in local therapy newspapers and magazines and had articles published in these, too.

Exercise 1—Client Analysis

You need to be able to answer the following about your target client group:

What are their ailments? _____

_____

What are their problems? _____

_____

Do you have rapport with them? _____

_____

Can you solve their problem? _____

_____

What do they want (as opposed to need)? _____

_____

Why do they want this service? _____

_____

What are their top values? _____

_____

Which values do you share? _____

_____

What are the top features of your service? _____

_____

How do those features benefit the client's needs and fit in with their values? _____

_____

Do you have the right qualifications and experience? _____

_____

Are you offering value for money? _____

_____

Are you open and available when they require the service? _____

_____

Do you offer a good service? _____

_____

What are their concerns with your service? _____

_____

How do you overcome those concerns? _____

_____

What messages will they respond to? _____

_____

*Further information to hone in on "*Who is your client?*"*

What gender are they? _____

_____

What age are they? _____

_____

What is their lifestyle? _____

_____

What is their income? _____

_____

What are their time constraints? _____

_____

Where do they shop? _____

_____

What are their hobbies and interests? _____

_____

Where do they go to do their hobbies or interests? _____

_____

What do they read? _____

_____

Which magazines or newspapers do they read? _____

_____

What do they watch on TV or listen to on the radio? _____

_____

What makes them feel important or needed? _____

_____

Who do they associate with? _____

_____

What really irritates them? _____

_____

Do they have children? _____

_____

What would appeal to them? _____

_____

Where do they live? _____

_____

What kind of housing? _____

_____

What car do they drive? _____

_____

Where do they go on holiday? _____

_____

For all customers (and we do the same!),whether they admit it or not, people want to know, "what's in it for me?". In other words they want to know what the benefits are to solve *their* particular problem, not the super whizzo features that you might want to sell to them. Tony Robbins, perhaps the most successful life coach and motivational speaker, says that people will do much more to get rid of pain rather than have additional pleasure. They will do a lot more to try and recover the £1000 they lost rather than spend out a thousand pounds on something that they would like.

You may consider that the services you provide have certain features, but the customers are interested in the benefits to them...

Feature: what you have on offer	Benefit to Customer: what they are interested in
take credit cards	flexible, convenient, can suit their budget
early, late, or weekend appointments	more choice, fits in around their lifestyle and work
approved technique/ accredited member of Institute	they can be guaranteed you know the technical aspects of your therapy and have the appropriate skills, and therefore can be trusted
easy or free parking	convenient, accessible, stress-free, good for the budget
fluffy towels, nice flowers, soft music	relaxation, pampering, "millionaire lifestyle"
appear on TV/ on Institute committee	you are committed to your profession, and you are an expert
wide range of services	choice, one-stop shop, accessible, trust
established and experienced	service, reliability, track record

You can insert your own here:

Feature: what you have on offer		Benefit to Customer: what they are interested in

Exercise 2—Self analysis

In all of your marketing, whether it is direct or indirect, you also need to know about yourself, and be able to answer:

Who am I? _____

_____

What is my strength? _____

_____

What is my niche? _____

_____

What is my knowledge? _____

_____

How do I help my clients? _____

_____

It is important that you talk about what you are passionate about and get excited over, and tap into that with your clients. Being aware of your fears around your service will also help you to pinpoint if you are not being 100% committed, or are holding yourself back:

List down below all the reasons people should *not* buy from you (for example, you're recently qualified, not very good at business, don't know all the areas or ailments, think money is dirty, can't deal with confrontation...)

- _____
- _____
- _____
- _____
- _____

Against each of these fears you need to explore what evidence there is your fear is *not* true, and what other things you can do to get around this.

For example, if you have just qualified, this means you are up to date with all the latest techniques and facts, and that your training was rigorous and covered a number of case studies. If you feel you are not very good with business, the evidence is that you are working on that, by reading books such as this, attending courses, or retaining the services of those who can help you, for example an accountant or solicitor.

How Do You Attract Clients?

As I said earlier you do not want to chase clients, you want to attract them. In order to understand how to attract your clients you need to understand them more. Do this by asking about themselves when they phone or come through the door. When they approach, ask them how you can help.

People like talking about themselves so ask some questions about themselves, preferably open questions: *How did you ...? What are you looking for?*

Listen to their replies. When you find what their concerns and problems are, then (and only then) you can state how the benefits of the features of the service will help to resolve their problems.

As soon as they ask questions it is a sign that they are interested. This might be the time to try the "alternative close": "Would you prefer such and such a date or the week after?" It is important that you look after them and address their concerns.

In the brilliant book by Robert Cialdini et al, *Yes! 50 Scientifically Proven Ways To Be Persuasive*, they look at the science behind persuasion. They suggest a variety of effective and ethical persuasion strategies, and pinpoint six universal principles of social influence:

1. **Reciprocation**. We tend to feel obligated to return favours performed for us. It is for this reason that quite often people will offer a free session, or book, or oils in the first instance to entice people to take up the service.
2. **Authority**. We look outside ourselves to external experts, particularly when we have a particular problem or concern. Thus when a car is broken down we take it to the garage; where we have a lot of emotional problems we book ourselves in for a series of sessions with a psychotherapist.
3. **Commitment/consistency**. We want to act consistently with our commitments and values.
4. **Scarcity**. The less available a resource, the more we want it. Hence you see a lot of offers "for a limited time only."
5. **Liking**. The more we like people, the more we want to say yes to them. It is for this reason that you need to build rapport and a long-term relationship with your customers.
6. **Social proof**. We look to what others do to guide our behaviour. It is for this reason that Amazon shows bestsellers. In the book, Cialdini cites the example of how changing the call to action in a television advert—from, "Call now on this number..." to, "If operators are busy, please call again"—resulted in a 26% increase in

people calling the hotline. People thought if it was busy then it
must be okay!

I strongly recommend that you get a hold of a copy of this book, *Yes! 50 Scientifically Proven Ways to Be Persuasive.*

If your toes are curling at this point, and you say you do not want to manipulate people, that it feels against your value system, I know where you're coming from! However, it is something that we actually do naturally: we like to give, whether it is a gift, time or money, and although we may think we are doing it for altruistic reasons, we are usually looking for something in return, even if it is only a smile or acknowledgement from a loved one. We do seek the services of experts when we need to find an answer. We also like to live and work consistently with our values. In fact one of the biggest causes of stress is when we are not acting in accordance with our values. (For a great treatise on this, do explore the book *Authentic*, by Neil Crofts.) Similarly, we are prepared to pay more for something that we consider to be special or rare or a "once-in-a-lifetime" opportunity. We naturally build rapport with people, as we like to be liked. Also, if we have difficulty booking an appointment with a particular therapist our natural reaction is to think "they must be good, because they are so busy"—and the converse!

So I recommend that you think about why people buy, and what you can do to encourage people to buy your services.

For a free copy of an e-book on how to promote your therapy services, go to this website: http://www.wellbeingbusinesssecrets.com/. Rebecca Keppel has some really useful tips and suggestions for helping to increase the number of customers and clients to your business.

Bonus Extra Tips To Help Increase Your Sales And Obtain More Customers

1. Give talks to local Women's Institutes, Business Link Breakfast Clubs and other associations, including a short demo (I've even

seen this work with a short counselling session which was very effective, and it gave the potential clients the opportunity to raise their concerns and objections and have them answered).

2. Do demos in offices. One ex-student persuaded her employer that once a month she would provide reflexology sessions to her co-workers, and would still be paid as normal by the company. She gained in that she obtained extra clients, raised her profile, and was paid her normal rate! The company gained as it could show to its employees that they cared about their health and explored ways to reduce stress levels.

3. Do demos in shopping malls. This is particularly helpful for set-ting up massage. By offering a free five-minute session and giving people the opportunity to win a series of six sessions if they leave their name and contact details including email, the therapist can follow up those contacts, even if they haven't won the main prize, and suggest they can have one free session or reduced rate ses-sion, if they book a course of six sessions.

4. Write articles, blog, or book. As noted above, being an author gives you a certain credibility and you're seen as the expert.

5. When you have something noteworthy to say, write a press re-lease. Press releases and editorials are by far the best way to get published in newspapers or magazines. People do not necessarily believe the claims made in advertisements, but they do believe editorial.

6. Contact your local GP surgery, local health centre, and other thera-pists. Write a letter introducing yourself and offer to meet up and follow up with a phone call or offer them the sessions they receive themselves.

7. Put up your leaflets or leave your business card in health food shops, pharmacists and other relevant shops.

8. Take a stall at an exhibition or festival. As these tend to be hard work and expensive, it is often a good idea to share the cost with other therapists and when you're busy, more than one of you could be working, and when you are not busy one person can

cover and the rest can go and look around the exhibition or festival and network as appropriate.

9. Create a newsletter that is circulated around your clients. This can be in paper form, or more typically nowadays via email. The newsletter gives information that is of use to the potential customer. Put a cover price on the front page of at least one pound and send a newsletter free with your compliments as this adds perceived value.

10. Keep updated contact records and contact clients once a year and ask how they are getting on and offer them a reduced rate on their "MOT" or update session.

11. Form strategic alliances with other practices.

12. Set up a website and have an online marketing strategy. This will be covered in **Module 11**.

Summary and Conclusions

Marketing is perhaps the most important part of running a successful business. It is also often the most neglected, with insufficient effort and time put onto it. If you plan your marketing strategy, measure the results, and apply that strategy on a longer-term basis, you have a much better chance of having a successful business.

Of course when you have done the marketing, you then need to deliver on the promises!

Module 11:
Communication
Website and Internet Marketing

．
．
．
．

A lot of students ask me, "Do I really need a website?" I know that some therapists believe they do not need to have a presence on the Internet, particularly if their target market is in the older age bracket. But with over 60 per cent of households in the UK now having broadband internet, and that figure growing each year, *not* to have a website is missing out on a real opportunity to grow your business to its full potential.

Website

95% of websites do not make money. A lot of therapy websites in particular are very pretty, complete with relaxing music and whirling chakras, but they are not particularly useful if people don't know that they are there and they're not covering the cost of their development. It is also missing out on a real opportunity for making your website not just a "bolt-on" to your business but a key part of your total marketing strategy. The problem is, a lot of web designers are not necessarily marketeers, or interested in marketing online.

You can have a very simple website that is very effective.

I have done a lot of research into Internet marketing, and one of the best courses I have found that shows you step-by-step how to do things online is by Neil Asher, who gives you lots of detail and lots of value. If you are serious about your business I recommend that you go to his website and check it out: http://www.neilasher.com

At the very least you need a landing page (or squeeze page, as this is sometimes called) where people can opt in for a free e-book/course/ article with lots of detailed information. On this page you give them lots of information, and you can take basic details from them, for example, their first name and email address.

Why do you need a page where people can opt in for further information or a free download? Many people don't trust the Internet, and it will therefore take between seven and ten contacts before people will begin to trust you. Most will not buy on first contact; having a contact address means that you can start building a relationship with them, rather than them leaving your site forever. Under the laws of reciprocation, if people feel they have been given something of real value, they are more likely to feel obliged to return the favour and sign up. Further, if they feel they are getting real value they will be clamouring to find out more and may eventually buy from you.

You can send out emails on a regular basis, or videos that you have prepared in advance. For example, you can send out information about how your therapy can help people using your target market. The great thing is that once you have set it up, you do not have to send things out each time; you can go through an automatic system that sends out a series of emails after a number of days. These automatic emails are called auto responders, which you can get from businesses such as http://www.aweber.com/ or http://www.totalbusinesscart.com

When people fill out the information or visit your premises, ask for their email address. Follow up their visit or request information with an email, perhaps offering them an "email exclusive" voucher.

Opportunities for affiliation

You can sell other people's products: either information—such as e-books, videos and audio downloads—or products. Find something that you truly believe in and you can passionately support, particularly if it helps clients with their problems. Through the affiliation you can earn commission.

Write blogs, articles and books to sell or give away

If you do giveaways remember to insert your full contact details and link back to your website. Links back to your website will be picked up by the search engines and tend to push up your ranking.

Choose your domain name carefully

Preferably register a name to do with your main niche. If you are a massage therapist specialising in rugby players why not get massageforrugbyplayers.com or massageforrugbyplayers.co.uk. If you want to be very localised you could have massageforrugbyplayersbristol. com, for example.

Use keywords in the website pages

Google and other search engines keep their algorithms secret. Algorithms are the ways in which they work out what should be higher up the rankings. They will look at relevancy, that is, whether pages seem relevant, linking in with what people have searched for (called keywords). Insert into your website (or ask your Webmaster to insert) your top five keywords in your title header in your website. Your keywords will be driven by what people might search for. Ask your Webmaster to show you Google Analytics, www.google.com/analytics/, which shows how keywords are searched for and how popular they are by region and town.

Make sure there is a link to the whole keyword phrase for example "Bristol Jungian analyst" not just "analyst", otherwise it will bring up all sorts of analysts, from psychoanalysts to business analysts!

Search engine optimisation

In order to be seen in the search engines (such as Google) and by people searching on your keywords, you need to appear in the first two pages of results of a search. You need to make your keywords and domain name specific to your niche, for example bristolreflexologist.com.

Link with other websites with relevant content and to your Institute website and make sure there is a reciprocal link so that you are listed as one of their approved practitioners.

Because a lot of therapists do not have websites, an effective website can bring a lot of potential clients—particularly younger clients, or busy executives. It is thought as many as 70 per cent of new clients can be achieved through an effective website.

As with all marketing you should test where you are getting your leads from, so on the website is possible to track where leaders come from, again using Google Analytics. Ask your Webmaster to ensure that this is included in your web pages.

Send out emails to your client list at least once a year, including old clients. Sometimes you have just dropped from people's memories. Perhaps you could offer an "MOT" or follow-up session.

Other tactics

Join forums, where people have problems make comments that are valuable and link back to your website.

Where people do have problems these queries are perfect for articles to be written which can be distributed through various magazine distributors, for example e-zines.

You can also write up information onto a blog. A good one to go for is Google's Blogger, as not surprisingly, Google tends to favour its own blog! See http://www.blogger.com/

For building up lists of people with similar interests it is worth using networking sites such as Facebook and Twitter, ensuring that in your interests, you include your keywords and your niche market.

As noted before for a very detailed step-by-step approach I suggest you look at the Neil Asher YouTube videos, and download some free stuff he has on the website http://www.neilasher.com

Summary and Conclusions

A website gives people information about your business, and a well-crafted, effective website can make you money. You can choose!

Module 12:
Keeping Score
Record-keeping and Accounts

Why Do You Need To Keep Records?
You need to keep records for a number of reasons, including:

a)   to substantiate what is in the accounts, which will be used by investors and bankers to measure how your business is doing;

b)   to prepare accounts for use in your tax return. If the accounts cannot be backed up by written documentation Her Majesty's Revenue and Customs (HMRC) will be able to challenge your figures more readily, and you may find yourself paying higher tax bills than you should;

c)   to keep accurate records to control the business and better plan for the future. An example of this may be that if you find your actual figures are considerably worse than your projections, you may need to reduce your drawings (salary that you paid yourself) in future months so that you do not go into a unauthorised overdraft with all the interest and penalty ramifications; and

d)   so that you can measure against your cash flow forecasts.

In Her Majesty's Revenue and Customs website they state that self-employed people must keep business records by law for 6 years after the end of the tax year to which the records relate. You can be charged £3000 for failure to maintain or retain records that you need to make your tax return. Also they state that you need to keep your business records and personal records separate and that most businesses find it helpful to have a separate business bank account.

Basic Records You Must Keep

Your basic records should include the following:

a) A record of all your sales, with copies of any invoices you have issued, or a receipt book in the case of a cash business such as therapy;

b) A record of all your business purchases and expenses;

c) Invoices and bills for all your business purchases and expenses unless they are for a very small amount. For VAT a "very small amount" is considered to be less than £100 but for income tax purposes and your own cash control purposes you may want to keep that down to less than £10. (See separate section on **Petty Cash** as I recommend keeping tally of even the smallest amounts).

d) Business stock or assets that you've taken out of the business (for your personal use) or put into the business.

e) Copies of business bank statements.

From the basic records you can draw up lists of all your income and all your expenditure. The lists of your income and expenditure are usually kept in one place called the "Cash Book" (which is actually a misnomer, as in reality it reflects what is going into and out of your bank account). To compare with the bank statements you receive you will also need to include the opening bank balance and by deducting the net outflows, or add the net inflows you can calculate the closing bank balance. See the **Bank Reconciliations** section later on.

You also need to deal with petty cash in some way and I will recommend a system on **page 131**. From the cashbook you, or an accountant, can draw up a set of accounts, which will be used as a basis for your tax return.

Companies

For companies there are more restrictions in terms of the level of accounting required. For example, companies need to keep detailed records of their capital equipment, that is, the assets that you use in the business (such as a car, or massage table or property). For accounts purposes, the cost of capital assets are spread over a number of years depending on the expected useful life of those assets. A massage table may last for five years before you have to replace it. Therefore, you spread the cost of the massage table over five years in your profit and loss account. For tax purposes there are special rules that relate to how much you're allowed to offset each year, these are called capital allowances (and in the UK they have changed recently – details can be found on the HMRC website).

Money coming in

Money coming, **income**, is also sometimes called turnover, and it includes all fees earned, sales and any other money you receive through the business.

Money going out

Costs are split into direct and indirect costs. **Direct costs** are those costs needed specifically to provide the service or sell the product. Examples are purchases i.e. the cost of raw materials and stock needed, and room rental, where rental is by the hour, massage oils for massage therapists and couch roll. **Indirect costs** (expenses, overheads) for example heating bills, insurance, subscriptions, telephone bills and room rental where it is a fixed cost, i.e. you have it for a day a week or longer.

Long-term (capital) assets are those items that you use to carry on your business, for example a car, computer, furniture, and massage table. The cost of these should be spread over their useful life.

"Drawings" is the term used for the money you personally take out of the business as a salary.

Other terms that you will need to know are:

Gross profit is total income minus direct costs.

Net profit is total income less all direct and indirect costs before drawings are taken out. Your taxable income will be based on the net profit before drawings are taken out. In other words the taxable income is based on the profits that the business is made not how much you have paid yourself. (Otherwise you could manipulate the amount you paid yourself, and the tax authorities don't like that!)

General Tips on Bookkeeping

1. Keep a system that works for you. The minimum that you need is a way of recording all your sales, what goes in and out of your bank account, and a petty cash system. As a therapist you should be operating a cash based system—not giving credit to your customers—so you may not need invoices. However, if you do raise invoices (I know a lot of psychotherapists like to raise invoices at the beginning of each month when the customer pays) or have a receipts book, you will need to number them sequentially and also keep copies of them all for the tax authorities.

2. Keep all your receipts, preferably in weekly or monthly order in a lever arch file. If you absolutely hate filing you can get away with putting everything on to a spike, which will at least keep them in some order until you write up the accounts. *Don't* do what my uncle used to do (he was a farmer who hated "bean counters"): he threw all his receipts and invoices into a cupboard and the accountant would come at the end of the year and the whole lot would spill out of the cupboard. The accountant then took hours trying to sort through the receipts to put them into some semblance of order before he could write up the books. It is not surprising the accounting bills were huge!

3. Open a separate bank account. Nowadays you can get online business accounts that don't charge for each transaction.

4. Do the bookkeeping (writing up the books) regularly.

5. Set aside about 30 per cent of your income to cover costs of tax and National Insurance that you need to pay. If necessary put it into a separate savings account. Tax is paid twice a year and

there is nothing more stressful than realizing that you don't have enough cash to pay the tax bill.

6. Money coming in: record money coming in on a sales sheet, also known as a sales daybook. You can use your appointment book as long as you cover the following information. Keep a listing of income as follows: date, name of client, amounts paid, date paid into the bank and whether it was cash or cheque. Add up the income each week, or daily if you see a lot of clients in the week. For security and control purposes it is good practice to go to the bank every few days.

7. Money going out: keep all your business receipts and make a note of how much money you've taken out of the business account. When you write up the accounts don't forget any bank payments, interest and charges.

Petty Cash

For small amounts of cash that don't go through the bank account I recommend something called an imprest system. You withdraw cash from the bank—a fixed amount, say £50—to cover your petty cash expenses. It is worth getting a petty cash tin in which to keep the cash.

Whenever you pay out anything by way of petty cash you either insert the receipt you receive or you write the cost on a piece of paper (or a petty cash receipt) and put the paper in the petty cash tin. At any one time you should have either cash or vouchers (which is a posh word for the receipts or bits of paper) that total £50.

When you are running short of cash in the petty cash tin you take out cash from the bank to cover the vouchers that you have paid out. These vouchers should be numbered and kept together and written up in the books when the amount is refreshed from the bank account. I tend to put the month and then order the vouchers numerically to keep track of them.

Monthly accounts

At the end of each month (or more frequently if you have a busy therapy business) you need to write up the books.

The first one is the cashbook. Record all the money going out of your bank account in the month by cheque, direct debit, bank transfer or standing order. Insert the date the payment was made. To track each cheque paid you will need to insert the cheque reference number, although you only need to use the last three numbers, as well as the total amount.

Where you have received an invoice, if you are not VAT registered the whole amount including VAT should be shown in the payments out.

Add up all the amounts you have paid out of the bank account in the month. This represents the total expenditure of the month.

Include all the money received into the bank account from your sales sheet, and any other payments in, for example if you receive bank interest. Add up all the amounts you have received in the month. This represents the total receipts received in the month.

The net "cash" inflow or outflow of the month will be the monthly receipts minus the monthly expenditure. This figure should be compared with the bank statement. The process is called a bank reconciliation.

Bank Reconciliation

Bank statements are sent out monthly and show the opening bank balance, the payments in and out of the account and the closing bank balance that will be carried forward to the following month.

You need to check that the balance at the end of the month in your cashbook agrees with that in your bank statement. Don't panic if the figures are not the same! This is where you need to check the differences.

What sort of differences are there?

Some cheques you have written will not have been paid in by the recipient yet and there may be deposits that have not yet cleared in the bank statement.

There may be transactions that are on the bank statement which have not been included in the cash book, for example standing orders, interest and bank charges. If they are correct they should be entered into the cashbook.

To agree (or "reconcile") the two balances the following procedure should be followed:

If the account on the bank statement is in credit (a positive bank balance), deduct from the statement balances any cheques issued that have not been presented and add any deposits made not recorded on the statement.

If the account is overdrawn add to the bank statement balance any cheques issued but not presented and deduct any deposits made.

If there is still a difference it means that there is something missing from either the cashbook or bank statement so I'm afraid there is nothing for it but to check off one against the other until you find the difference.

On the payments side of the cashbook it is really useful to use additional columns (called analysis columns) that are headed with descriptions, which can be used to categorise expenditure, for example travel, stationery, postage etc. This applies whether you do the accounts manually or have set up a spreadsheet.

Ideally the headings should correspond with those used in the profit forecast, cash flow forecast and tax return (it makes it easier to compare the figures). The analysis columns should be totalled at the end of the month and compared with the expected amounts shown in the financial projections prepared at the start of the trading period (in other words in the cash flow forecast).

Filing

File all of your receipts and bills in month order.

Preparing Accounts

At the end of the year the various analysis columns for each month should be added up to give a total figure for the year for each of the categories. The sales income for the year should be totalled up and the difference between the two should be the profit before any depreciation. Add back any expenditure on capital assets (such as computers) and deduct the depreciation (the wear and tear on the assets) to arrive at your net profit before drawings figure. This set of figures will be used as a basis for your tax returns. Adjustments will be items that are not allowable for tax—see **Examples of non-allowable expenditure in Module 13**.

Employees

Throughout this book, I have assumed that you do not have any employees. However, if you do, your record keeping needs to be even more meticulous: you need to record all the payments you have made to your employee(s), the amount that you have deducted for income tax, any deductions (such as student loans) and National Insurance from the employee and you will also need to calculate and record the employer's National Insurance. You will need information about fixed assets such as cars, equipment or property, which will always need to be recorded. As employer you are a tax collector for the government and you will need to record the tax you have withheld from every employee under the Pay As You Earn (PAYE) system and you will need to pay over the tax and National Insurance to Her Majesty's Revenue and Customs on a monthly or quarterly basis.

Wages Records

You have certain legal duties towards your employees and these include giving an itemised pay statement showing the tax and national insurance contributions taken from their salaries and wages under the pay as you earn scheme. You must keep the following information for employees:

- Name and address
- National Insurance number
- Pay As You Earn reference number
- Gross pay
- Pension deductions
- Student loan deductions and any other deductions authorised by the employee, for example union fees

The actual individual's wages records need to show:

- Gross pay including bonuses and tips
- Pension contributions
- Total pay to date
- Tax-free pay to date (see the Employers CD sent out to you as an employer or the online support from the HMRC website which do these calculations for you)
- Taxable pay to date
- Tax due to date (see online information for the calculator)
- Tax paid to date
- Tax due on earnings for this period (since the start of the income tax year)
- Employees' National Insurance contributions for this period
- Other deductions
- Net pay
- Employer's National Insurance contributions

- Any statutory sick pay, all statutory maternity pay, student loan payments.

In the UK the tax year runs from 6 April in one year to 5 April in the next.

VAT

You are required to keep separate VAT accounts if you are registered for VAT. The current **turnover** threshold (i.e. not profit) you have to achieve before you must register for VAT is (in Autumn 2009) £68,000. This changes annually, so check the HMRC website, http://www.hmrc.gov.uk/vat/forms-rates/rates/rates-thresholds.htm#2.

If you are registered for VAT, in your cash book you should show the amount of sales including VAT, the amount of VAT charged, the total amount of purchases including VAT and the amount of VAT paid. The difference between the VAT charged on the sales and the VAT paid on purchases broadly represent the VAT you need to pay to Her Majesty's Revenue and Customs. Most therapists do not reach the turnover threshold for having to register for VAT, so I have not included this further.

Summary and Conclusions

You need to keep records and accounts to control the business and for tax purposes. The key to success here is to find a system that works for you (whether it is manual or on computer) and do the books regularly to keep in control of the business and make any adjustments if necessary if the actual figures are not as good as the proposed figures.

Module 13: Pay Your Dues

An Introduction to
Income Tax for the Self-Employed

.
.
.
●

The information given here is of a general nature and shall not con-
stitute giving tax or legal advice. It should help by pointing you in the
right direction so you can get the most up-to-date information from the
HMRC website or so you can talk to your accountant about the issues
raised. It is based on the UK rules in effect at the end of 2009.

Registering for Tax and National Insurance

The majority of therapists are either in business as sole traders (on
their own) or in partnership (with others). The tax rules for sole traders and partnerships are similar.

As a sole trader or partnership you must notify Her Majesty's Revenue
and Customs (HMRC) that you have started trading, within 90 days of
commencement of trading.

The trouble is when do you start trading, in reality?

Until you are qualified you are not legally allowed to trade, and usually
under the rules of your governing bodies you are not allowed to accept
payment for your services. So the earliest that you can commence trading for tax purposes is when you are fully qualified, and you have your
appropriate insurances and certificates.

Her Majesty's Revenue and Customs will try and say that you are starting trading as early as possible, so they can tax you as early as possible! Sometimes having a small advert in a newsagents is sufficient evidence for the Revenue to say that you are trading.

The Revenue will look at what they call "the badges of trade," i.e. what you would expect a business to do. Examples include sending out flyers or leaflets, setting up a bank account or receiving the first paying client. As you may have gathered there is no hard and fast rule about when you start trading. It may be in your interest to show that you do start trading before you make a profit, for although you will have to account to the Revenue for the income that you have received, you will be able to offset some of the costs that you have incurred.

National Insurance

In addition to paying income tax, a sole trader or partnership must pay two sorts of National Insurance contributions, called Class 2 and Class 4 National Insurance contributions. **Class 2 National Insurance contributions** are payable at a fixed rate per week, currently £2.40 per week. If profits are below a certain limit, £5,075 in 2009/2010, you can claim not to have to pay Class 2 National Insurance (it is not automatic, you need to claim—for details see the HMRC website). For the latest limits and rates see http://www.hmrc.gov.uk/rates/nic.htm

Class 4 National Insurance is taxable as a percentage of profits. Class 4 National Insurance does not entitle you to any benefits in the UK.

Tax Calculations

In practice the business hardly ever pays tax on the exact profit figure shown in the accounts. You have to make adjustments for the following reasons.

Taxation is based on the net profits before "drawings" (what you take as salary) from the business. Additionally some business expenses are not allowed to be offset against your tax charge, for example entertaining and gifts costing more than £50, and some costs are only allowed in part where they are used partly for business. The only allowable part for tax purposes is the business element.

Generally, long-term assets (such as computers) are not allowed against tax as a lump sum in the year. Some (but not all) long term assets are allowed by costs being spread over a number of years by way of capital allowances, which are set by HMRC (the best explanation is probably on the Business Link website: see their page on capital allowances at http://tinyurl.com/capital-allowances).

The rates of income tax and national insurance and capital allowances change regularly each year. See http://www.hmrc.gov.uk/rates/it.htm for details.

Examples of allowable expenditure:

- oils and other goods bought for resale
- wages and salaries
- advertising and promotion
- hire of therapy equipment
- room rental
- insurance
- interest on business loans. If you take out a mortgage and you can demonstrate that the loan has been used exclusively for the purpose of the business (for example to buy some assets in the business) then you can offset the interest element of that part of the mortgage against your tax bill.
- repairs to plant machinery
- VAT, where trade is not registered for VAT and therefore unable to claim the VAT

- administrative costs including business rates, telephone, stationery, postage, heating and lighting (including the business element of your home fuel bills if you work at home)
- professional fees including accounting and legal fees—but not tax advice!
- travel on business trips and the costs of running cars used in the business, although any non-business element will need to be excluded
- some training costs where those are incidental to the business. For example a one-day seminar is allowable, but a homoeopathic practitioner course would not be allowable as it would be considered to be a long-term asset and is not eligible for capital allowances. It may help to think of long-term assets as those that enable you to carry out your business, in this example, the training course carried out to enable you to set up as a homeopath. Generally, ongoing training courses related to keeping you up to date in the same business, for example any requirements for continuing professional development, are allowable.
- subscriptions to professional bodies needed for the business
- owner's pension contributions, subject to certain limits.

Examples of non-allowable expenditure:
- personal or domestic expenditure
- stock taken for personal use in the business
- personal drawings (the amount you pay yourself as salary)
- entertaining expenses
- depreciation of assets
- illegal fines such as parking tickets
- travel from home to work. The exception to this is if your home is your ordinary place of work.
- business gifts costing more than £50.

For more details of the taxation of the self employed see the HMRC website: http://www.hmrc.gov.uk/incometax/relief-self-emp.htm#3

Additionally, everybody is allowed a personal allowance each year in the UK. This is a slice of tax-free income that you can offset against all your income for the year, including that from the business.

Summary and Conclusions

Taxation is country-specific and changes each year. It is therefore critical that you research the latest position by reading the relevant websites, such as the HMRC, www.hmrc.gov.uk, and the Business Link website, www.businesslink.gov.uk.

Module 14:
Ready for Take-off
Planning and Checklists

•
•
•
•

The good news...

If you got this far, well done!

The bad news...

That's the easy bit.

Before you can set up in business there are certain things that you need to have checked that you have done and you need to plan for those accordingly. One way to plan is to prepare what is called a "milestone plan".

Milestone Plan
This is really just a list of the activities that you need to do; how long you think each one is going to take; and what the outcome or "**deliverable**" is—by that I mean, for example, if the activity is to choose a business name then the deliverable of the output is "business name decided". These key decision points or deliverables are called "**milestones**" and signify important progress towards the goal.

You need to specify:
- the duration that you expect the activity will take
- the start date of the activity and the date by which something has to be completed (this may be longer than the duration)
- if more than one person is involved in the process, state the person responsible for the delivery of that activity
- notes of any details that may be relevant.

The lists should be broadly chronological, and you'll need to highlight those items that can start before you have completed an earlier activity.

Checklists

Just as pilots have to undertake a series of checks before they can take off, I recommend that you go through the following checklists to ensure that you have all the items covered—or you know where you can get the information—before you start.

I have kept them simple, with a quick **yes/no** answer. Answer them quickly: your instinctive answer is the usually the best one. The intention is to have an overwhelming number of **yes** answers. Some of the questions seem to be repeated: this is deliberate! Where you answer **no** I recommend you assess how you are going to get around them and how important that **no** is to you.

Checklist 1: It's All About You

Can you work long hours on things that interest you?	○yes ○no
Are you a self-starter, someone who does not need pushing or supervision?	○yes ○no
Do you have persistence and stamina?	○yes ○no
Are you the sort of person who frequently comes up with new ideas to get around problems?	○yes ○no
Do you do things differently if the first option doesn't work?	○yes ○no
Are you willing to do without holidays and spare time?	○yes ○no

Do you have support from your friends and family, who do
not object to you putting in those extra hours? ○yes ○no

If your business were to struggle in three years, would you
keep going? ○yes ○no

Do you see problems as challenges? ○yes ○no

Do you set yourself goals, and gain satisfaction from
achieving them? ○yes ○no

Can you work alone and are you happy to do so? ○yes ○no

Can you live without job security and a regular income? ○yes ○no

Do others consider you to be a good all-rounder? ○yes ○no

Do you analyse your performance so that you can do
something better next time? ○yes ○no

Are you good at finding the right person or resources to help
you get what you want? ○yes ○no

Do you recognise and acknowledge when you need help? ○yes ○no

Have you got over your fears and concerns and discovered
what has held you back in the past? ○yes ○no

Can you delegate to others? ○yes ○no

Is your health good? ○yes ○no

Do you set your own standards to compete against? ○yes ○no

Do you feel really comfortable about money and business and
that you will be adding value to your clients? ○yes ○no

Do you have a professional attitude towards your practice
and towards your business? ○yes ○no

Do you really, really want to set up in business on your own? ○yes ○no

Do you have a vision board of what success means to you in
business? ○yes ○no

Have you discussed your thoughts with your friends and
family about setting up in business? ○yes ○no

Have you worked out a revised budget to see how you will
cope, especially in the early months? ○yes ○no

Is the family supportive of you setting up in business,
and do they realise the implications? ○yes ○no

Are they able and willing to support and help around the
house, or indeed in the business itself, if necessary? ○yes ○no

Checklist 2: Skills and Knowledge

Have you thoroughly assessed your skills and knowledge?	○yes○no
Have you honestly and objectively worked out the strengths and weaknesses of yourself and your business?	○yes○no
Have you worked out how you are going to fill the gaps in your skills or knowledge base?	○yes○no
Have you ever successfully negotiated contracts with credit terms?	○yes○no
Are you comfortable drawing up cash flow forecasts and profit statements?	○yes○no
Are you happy to keep simple books, either manually or on the computer?	○yes○no
Are you comfortable asking people for money?	○yes○no
Do you understand the importance of controlling your cash flow?	○yes○no
Do you know how you are going to fund the business?	○yes○no
Do you know the breakeven point of your business?	○yes○no
Do you feel comfortable presenting your business plan?	○yes○no

Checklist 3: Planning and Regulations

Have you completed your business plan?	○yes○no
Have you presented it to other people to check its feasibility?	○yes○no
Have you completed your cash flow forecasts, and profit and loss forecasts?	○yes○no
Have you decided where you are going to set up business from?	○yes○no
Have you secured all the insurances you need?	○yes○no
Have you decided on a business name?	○yes○no
Have you checked that you comply with all local regulations?	○yes○no
Have you done a risk assessment?	○yes○no
Have you registered with Her Majesty's Revenue and Customs?	○yes○no
Have you registered with the VAT authorities, if necessary?	○yes○no

Have you secured premises or a rental of rooms? ○ yes ○ no

Have you applied for any licenses you need? ○ yes ○ no

Checklist 4: Market Research

Have you conducted market research on the market, to work
out the competition and the demand for services? ○ yes ○ no

For each of the niche markets that you will be providing
services to, can you describe the two main competitors? Their
proximity to your business premises? Their prices and key
selling points? ○ yes ○ no

Can you describe your unique selling proposition (USP)? ○ yes ○ no

Do you believe that you are the best person to provide this
particular service in your area? ○ yes ○ no

Do you have a contingency funding plan in the case of
reduced sales income? ○ yes ○ no

Have you ascertained the level of demand? ○ yes ○ no

Do you have a clear view of your target market, and their
lifestyles? ○ yes ○ no

Can you describe in detail your target customers, their problems and how you are going to solve those problems? ○ yes ○ no

Have you found out how your target market will find out
information about services such as yours? ○ yes ○ no

Have you worked out how to communicate with your target
market in the most cost-efficient manner? ○ yes ○ no

Have you completed your marketing plan? ○ yes ○ no

Have you set your fee structure? ○ yes ○ no

Have you collected evidence that you can show of your
market being in growth, in decline or static? ○ yes ○ no

Have you signed up to various forums and websites that are
relevant to your target market? ○ yes ○ no

Have you created your marketing literature? ○ yes ○ no

Do you have a clear idea of your brand image and logo? ○ yes ○ no

Checklist 5: Financing

Have you applied to the providers of finance and secured the necessary funding?	○ yes ○ no
Have you checked your credit rating?	○ yes ○ no
Do you know exactly how much money you will need to set up?	○ yes ○ no
Do you have a contingency plan if your costs are higher and your income is lower in the first 12 months of operating?	○ yes ○ no
Have you considered all the hidden extras on setup, for example, sets of keys being cut, marketing literature, stationery and office supplies?	○ yes ○ no
Have you set up your bank account?	○ yes ○ no

Checklist 6: Policies

Have you set up a clear policy around	
payment?	○ yes ○ no
missed appointments?	○ yes ○ no
non-discrimination?	○ yes ○ no
data retention and use?	○ yes ○ no
Have you registered under the Data Protection Act?	○ yes ○ no
Have you created an ethical and environmental policy?	○ yes ○ no
Have you considered how you can buy from ethical suppliers?	○ yes ○ no

Checklist 7: Website

Have you set up your website?	○ yes ○ no
Have you joined various forums that are relevant to your therapy business?	○ yes ○ no
Do you have a blog?	○ yes ○ no
Do you have a database of potential customers?	○ yes ○ no
Have you considered whether you will write and disseminate articles?	○ yes ○ no
Have you considered what potential there is for affiliations?	○ yes ○ no

Have you considered what opportunities there are for selling other people's products? ○ yes ○ no

Do you know how to update your website on a regular basis? ○ yes ○ no

Checklist 8: Book-keeping and Accounts

Have you considered whether you need a bookkeeper? ○ yes ○ no

Have you considered whether you need an accountant? ○ yes ○ no

If the answer is yes, have you secured the services of an accountant and/or bookkeeper? ○ yes ○ no

Have you worked out how you are going to keep your books i.e. either manually or on the computer? ○ yes ○ no

Are your books set up and ready to go? ○ yes ○ no

Do you have your filing system set up? ○ yes ○ no

Do you have somewhere to keep your clients' records safe and secure? ○ yes ○ no

Checklist 9: Supervision and Professional Development

Have you organised a supervisor? ○ yes ○ no

Is there a peer-to-peer support system? If not, have you considered setting one up? ○ yes ○ no

Have you considered what ongoing professional development you need, when you will schedule this in and how much it will cost? ○ yes ○ no

Checklist 10: The Future

Do you have a clear idea of how you will grow your business in the future? ○ yes ○ no

Have you worked out your exit strategy? ○ yes ○ no

Have you worked out the risks of the business failing? ○ yes ○ no

Do you have contingency plans if the business fails? ○ yes ○ no

Have you worked out the opportunities of the business growing and being very financially successful? ○ yes ○ no

Do you have plans as to how to manage in the event of
being financially successful? ○ yes ○ no

Checklist 11: Success Criteria

Have you written down a clear statement of your criteria for
success in the business over the next year? ○ yes ○ no

Have you written down a number of smaller achievements
you wish to achieve, leading up to that success criterion? ○ yes ○ no

Do you know how you are going to help your customers? ○ yes ○ no

Summary and Conclusions

The checklist questions have been posed so that you should have a
majority of **yes** answers. Obviously you will need to decide which ones
are critical to have completed before you start business (for example,
obtaining insurance, licenses and access to premises, if you are not
going to be mobile), and which are "nice to have".

Conclusions

Well done for getting through this step-by-step guide to setting up a therapy business. We have covered a lot of ground and you should have a much clearer view of the steps that you need to take to set up a successful business.

Keep an eye on my website http://www.setupatherapybusiness.com for updates and additional resources, including the collection of "how to" videos which you can watch.

As I mentioned at the beginning, if there are particular aspects of setting up a business you would like me to cover, please email me at gefwarren@gmail.com and I will do what I can to cover it by way of blog or video as appropriate.

If you really want to make a difference to your business and would like the one-to-one business mentoring and coaching for your therapy business, where I metaphorically hold your hand (and hold you to account!) email me at the above address and ask about business mentoring.

Good luck!

Bibliography
Further reading

These are the books that I have found most useful when compiling this book, and I thoroughly recommend that you read them for further information:

Anderson, Chris. *The Long Tail: How Endless Choice is Creating Unlimited Demand*, 2006, Random House Business Books, London

Armato, Jenny. *Web Millionaire Secrets; Discover How to make YOUR First Million Online... and Make it Last!* 2009, GOKO Publishing, Sydney

Barclay, Liz, Colin Barrow, Paul Barrow, and Gregory Brooks. *Starting and Running a Business All-in-One for Dummies*, 2007, John Wiley & Sons, Chichester

Burns, Paul. *Entrepreneurship and Small Business* 2nd Ed., 2007, Palgrave Macmillan, Basingstoke

Gerber, Michael E. *The E-myth Revisited: Why Most Small Businesses Don't Work and What to Do About it* 3rd Edition, Harper Collins, London

Goldstein, Noah J, Steve J Martin & Robert B Cialdini. *Yes! 50 Scientifically Proven Ways to Be Persuasive* 2007, Profile Books, London

Masterson, Michael. *The Architecture of Persuasion: How to Write a Well Constructed Sales Letter* 2008, American Writers and Artists Inc, Delray Beach

Patten, Dave. *Successful Marketing for the Small Business* 2nd Edition, 1989, Daily Telegraph Guide/ Kogan Page, London

Rickman, Cheryl D. *The Small Business Start-Up Workbook: A Step by Step Guide to Starting the Business You've Dreamed Of* 2005, How To Books, Oxford

Williams, Sara. *Lloyds TSB Small Business Guide* 17th Ed., 2003, Vitesse Media, London

Websites

Setting up/ General

http://www.setupatherapybusiness.com

http://www.businesslink.gov.uk

http://www.lawsociety.org.uk/choosingandusing/helpyourbusiness/foryourbusiness.law

https://www.alliance-leicestercommercialbank.co.uk/bizguides/full/index.asp

http://www.companieshouse.gov.uk/

Local Market information

http://www.upmystreet.com

http://www.caci.com

For Market information and reports

http://www.keynote.co.uk

http://www.snapdata.com/index.php?module=search

http://uk.nielsen.com/site/index.shtml

http://reports.mintel.com/

Online Market Research

http://www.surveymonkey.com/

UK Tax Registration

http://www.hmrc.gov.uk/startingup/index.htm

http://www.hmrc.gov.uk/vat/forms-rates/rates/rates-thresholds.htm#2

Trade Mark registration (if appropriate)

http://www.ipo.gov.uk/

Health & Safety websites

http://www.fire.org.uk

http://www.hse.gov.uk

Other UK regulators

http://local.direct.gov.uk/LDGRedirect/Start.do?mode=1

http://www.ico.gov.uk/what_we_cover/data_protection/notification.
aspx

http://www.direct.gov.uk

http://www.ppluk.com/en/Music-Users/Playing-Music-and-Videos-In-
Public/

Money saving advice/ forms of funding

http://www.money-savingexpert.com

http://www.princeofwales.gov.uk/personalprofiles/theprinceofwales/
atwork/theprincescharities/opportunityandenterprise/

Marketing Therapy Businesses

http://www.wellbeingbusinesssecrets.com/freebook.html?utm_
source=affiliates&utm_medium=affiliates&utm_
campaign=free%2Breport

http://www.massagetherapymarketingsuccess.com/

Internet Marketing

http://www.neilasher.com

http://www.totalbusinesscart.com

Lightning Source UK Ltd.
Milton Keynes UK
UKOW04f0846010716

277400UK00008B/149/P